SALESFORCE FOR BUSINESS USERS

Mastering Salesforce Lightning platform to boost your productivity and work more efficiently.

Johan Yu

ISBN-13: 978-981-18-1953-7

To my wife Novida and my son Jeremy,
you are my world, my love.

CONTENTS

Foreword....7
About the Author....9
About the Technical Reviewer....11
Acknowledgment....13
Introduction....15
Chapter 1: Customizing My User Interface....17
Chapter 2: The Power of List View....35
Chapter 3: Collaborate with Chatter....55
Chapter 4: Searching the Data....73
Chapter 5: Reporting on the Cloud....87
Chapter 6: Advanced Reporting Features....111
Chapter 7: Building Dashboard....135
Chapter 8: Salesforce Mobile App....153
Appendix: Setting Up My Salesforce....169

FOREWORD

When I joined Equinix in 2017 as the head of Global Sales Operations, I was told that we had an SFDC 'Grand Master' on the team who had received numerous awards and was a published SFDC book author. Later, when I was able to meet Johan Yu in person and even celebrate with him virtually during Covid at the birth of his son Jeremy, did I learn more about the very thoughtful man, husband, and father.

Over time I have been witness to the impact that he has made for our organization through numerous strategic projects and initiatives, as well as through countless awards and accolades that he has received from people throughout the company. He is quite frankly known as a 'legend' throughout Equinix, and it is an honor to be able to intro this new book from him.

I start off with this context for Johan as this is surely not something that he would say about himself, as he is ever modest and continuously seeking to do more and do better. I had the good fortune to work at Salesforce in San Francisco years ago and can honestly say that he is a world-class category of SFDC architects, and we are extremely fortunate to have him working with us @ Equinix. I hope that you will enjoy the book and the insights for business users, from one who has the privilege of receiving them regularly from Johan himself!

Whitney Merrill,

Vice President, Global Sales Operations - Equinix

ABOUT THE AUTHOR

Johan Yu has more than 20 years of working experience in the IT sector across multiple industries and at a leading Salesforce consulting company.

He has spent more than 17 years working with Salesforce technology, starting his career as a Salesforce developer, consultant, and architect, among many other challenging roles.

Based in Singapore, Johan holds 15x Salesforce certifications, ranging from Administrator, Consultants to Architect/Designer certifications. Since 2013, he has led the Salesforce Singapore User Group and is active in the Trailblazers Community.

In May 2014, Johan become the first Salesforce MVP from Southeast Asia. Thanks to his contribution to the Tableau CRM community, Johan is awarded as the first batch of Tableau CRM Ambassadors in June 2019.

Johan is passionate about user experience and architecting solutions that make a system that works most simply and efficiently. In his spare time, he likes to learn and research new Salesforce technologies and sharing in his blog *www.simplysfdc.com*

ABOUT THE TECHNICAL REVIEWER

Rebecca Sweetman

Rebecca Sweetman started working as an 'accidental admin' in 2016 and became hooked. She has now been working in the Salesforce ecosystem for over 5 years and holds certifications in Admin, Advanced Admin, Sales Cloud Consulting and as a Pardot Specialist.

On her own learning journey, she noticed a lack of tools from a user's perspective, so took a keen interest in this project when approached.

Rebecca is a Kiwi based in Singapore and is a Senior member of the global Sales Operations team for a media tech company called Extreme Reach.

You can find her on Twitter or Instagram *@idosalesforce*

Jason Lim

Jason is a technology enthusiast who has been working on the Salesforce platform since 2009, starting the journey as a system administrator.

Over the years, he had also ventured into various roles such as the application developer, business analyst, project manager, and solution architect.

His diverse experience and strong interest in technology encourage him to build the best solutions with the latest Salesforce features.

Currently, he is the co-leader of Salesforce Singapore User Community Group. In 2020, he co-organized a community conference *https://singaporedreamin.com* with fellow community leaders and members.

He holds a bachelor's degree in Computer Science and works as an IT functional lead in Singapore.

ACKNOWLEDGMENT

I would like to take this opportunity to recognize and say thank you to everyone who directly and indirectly contributed to this book. Writing this book was quite a journey, and I am grateful for every opportunity, support, and feedback.

- My boss and teams: **Adrian**, **Eileen**, **John**, and **Swapna**, you guys are awesome, it is always a pleasure to work with all of you.
- My ex-boss: **Chris Varr** and **Henry Cheung**, thank you for the trust and opportunity given, wishing both of you an enjoyable retirement life.
- My VP of Global Sales Ops: **Whitney Merrill**, thank you for the leadership, and foreword for this book.
- My extended teams: **Daniel** and **Suki**, you guys always inspire me, and push me to keep learning.
- All Singapore Trailblazers, especially **Rebecca Sweetman** and **Jason Lim**, thanks for the friendship and support to Salesforce Singapore User Group in the last many years, and also as the technical reviewers of this book.
- My cell group **Singa-Indo**, thank you for always listening, support, and prayer to get this book completed.
- My Salesforce MVPs family, a group of smart and trusted resources.
- My Equinix family, a place where I grow and enjoy the most.
- Every trailblazer in the community, find your path and leave a trail.

INTRODUCTION

Firstly, thank you for acquiring this book. It is written especially for business users who are using or planning to use the Salesforce Lightning in their daily jobs, such as Sales, Sales Operations, Sales Support, Customer Service, Management, Marketing, Revenue, Commercial, Business Operations, Finance, Operations, or many other departments.

This book will focus on the Salesforce features, best practices, tips, and hands-on exercises. The knowledge earns from this guide will boost your overall productivity when working daily on the Salesforce platform, and your ability to make the most out of it.

You will find this guide less wordy than many. We use bullet points, handy tips, screenshots, and examples to get you hands-on so you can easily follow along and try to use the features mentioned on the spot, so you will retain the required information, and not waste time with unnecessary detail.

The background on why I write this book is because Salesforce has so many features and it is evolving, which is totally different from legacy systems, where features will only be available when you request to be built.

Salesforce has 3 releases per year with a lot of features are introduced for you to use in every release. However, as most of us are busy with our daily jobs, we never care and probably never been informed of the new releases and the features. This book is written to summarize all the latest and powerful features that will help you to be more productive.

Hope you will enjoy and learn new things from this book and be more productive!

CHAPTER 1:

CUSTOMIZING MY USER INTERFACE

The first chapter will focus on the Salesforce Lightning **user interface**, items that you can be customized, how to customize, and the benefits when you customize it.

Here are the main topics that we will go through:

- Selecting your display density
- Adding and accessing Favorites
- Personalizing the navigation bar
- Pinning list view in a tab
- Personalizing related list

Setting your display density

As we are working for many hours every day in front of our computer, we should ensure that our user interface is set up in a way that is comfortable to us, this will help us to be more productive and healthier.

Salesforce Lightning allows each user to adjust their display density as per user preference. There are two display density options offered by the Lightning platform: **Comfy** and **Compact**. We just need to select it once, and Salesforce will remember it for us for the future.

Let's look at each of the display density options, here is the page layout with Comfy density:

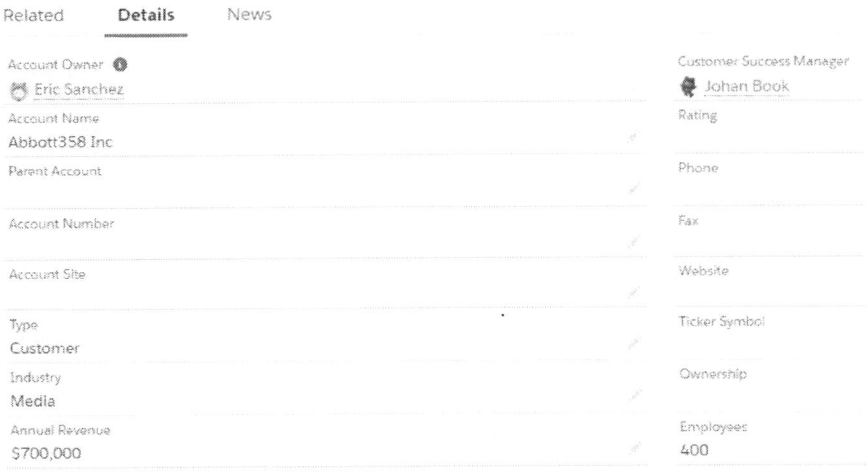

Figure 1.1 - Page layout with Comfy density

In the Comfy density, the field value is displayed below the field name, giving a larger gap between fields and thus more white space in your page layout than in the Compact density. *Figure 1.2* is the same layout as *Figure 1.1*, but displayed as Compact density:

Figure 1.2 - Page layout with Compact density

With Compact density, the field value is displayed after the field name, the screen has fewer white spaces and a shorter page layout.

Which one is better?

It depends on your personal preference, so there is no right or wrong option here. Some people say Comfy is more relaxed for our eyes, but feel free to test them both and decide which one suits you better.

The benefit of selecting Compact and if the page has a lot of fields, you need to scroll less to reach the bottom of the page, you need to scroll more if you select Comfy.

Best Practice

Select display density that fits you better, everyone has their different preference, so test both options, then stay to one of the options.

How to Change Display Density

It is easy to switch from Compact to Comfy, or from Comfy to Compact:

1. Click your avatar at the upper right corner of the Lightning page:

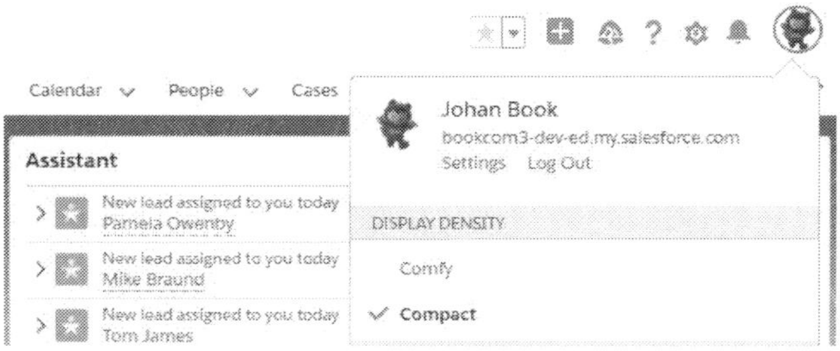

Figure 1.3 - Switching display density

2. Notice the option to select **Comfy** or **Compact** under **Display Density**. From here, you can select the option that you wish to use.
3. Once you select Comfy or Compact, the system will prompt you if you want to refresh the page, click the **Refresh Now** button. The display density will be updated for you.
4. You can always switch between Comfy or Compact to experience which display density is working better for you.

Working with Favorites

Favorites in Salesforce are similar to bookmarks in a web browser, it allows you to open a page or record in a single click. However, Favorites are much more powerful than browser bookmarks because they do not depend on a browser or device. You can access your Favorites items from any web browser and any device, including from the Salesforce mobile app, we will discuss the mobile app in *Chapter 6, Salesforce Mobile App*.

Your favorites are accessible from any pages in Salesforce Lightning, you can add any Salesforce Lightning record as a favorite, such as an Account, Contact, Report, Dashboard, and so on, including List View, we will discuss list view in *Chapter 2, The Power of List View*.

What are the benefits?

Favorites help you to access frequently used items easily, instead of wasting time in finding those items or records. Furthermore, to add or access items added as favorites are very easy and fast, so there is no harm in making use of this feature, which ultimately will help you in your daily tasks.

Of course, you can simply ignore Favorites in Salesforce, but adding the records that you use the most will save you time, such as searching for and running weekly reports, finding the right pipeline dashboards, or accessing leads and opportunities that need follow-up.

Managing Items in Favorites

The items in your Favorite list ideally should only contain items that you are working on, or use often. So, you should maintain the list regularly.

Adding a record to Favorites

To a record into Favorite is simple:

1. Open the record you would like to add as a favorite. For example, I am adding a Lead named 'Bertha Boxer' as a favorite, because I will be working on that Lead in the next few days or weeks.
2. Click the star icon at the upper right corner next to the search box:

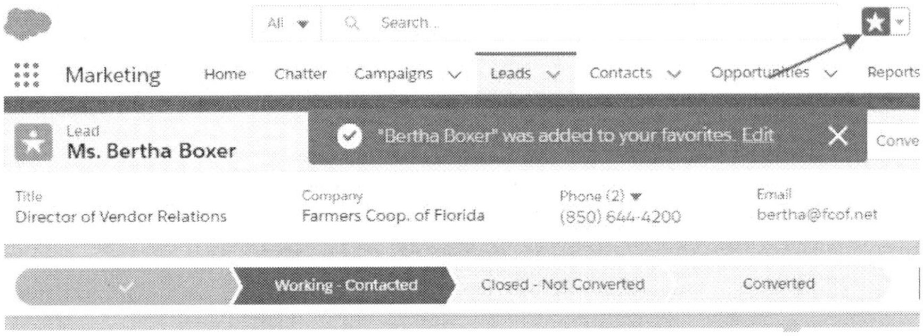

Figure 1.4 - Adding record as a favorite

3. Once added, the area surrounding the star icon becomes blue. This process is the same for any other type of record that you want to add to your favorites item.

> **Notes**
> As of now, you can have up to 200 items added to your favorite.

Removing item from Favorites

There are 2 ways to remove items from Favorite:

1. Open the record or list view that has been added as a favorite, notice the area surrounding the star icon is blue, then click the star icon to remove it from favorite, the area surrounding the icon will turn to gray.
2. Click the arrow next to the star icon, then click the pencil icon **Edit Favorites** link at the bottom of the window, you can remove items by clicking the cross icon at the end of each item. Click **Done** when finish.

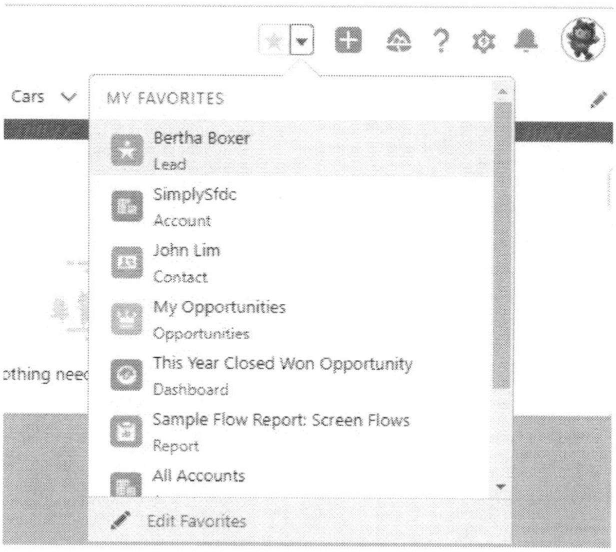

Figure 1.5 – List of Items in Favorites

Editing Favorites

Click the arrow next to the star icon, then click the pencil icon **Edit Favorites** link at the bottom of the window. In this window you can:

- Search an item added in Favorites from the search box
- Delete item from Favorites by clicking the cross icon
- Re-label items added in Favorites by clicking the pencil icon
- Re-order the list by drag-and-drop the item

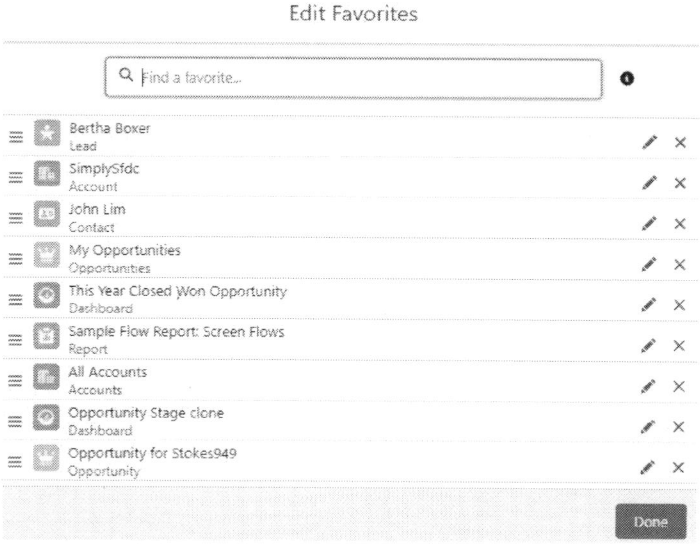

Figure 1.6 – Editing Favorites

Best Practice

You should maintain the number of records added as Favorites. This means that when you no longer work with a record (e.g., an opportunity has been closed), you should remove it from your favorites. Too many records added as favorites will make your favorites list unorganized and hard to navigate, which will defeat the purpose of the feature itself.

How to access Favorites?

As mentioned earlier, once a record is added as a favorite, you can access it from anywhere in Salesforce Lightning, including Salesforce mobile app. This includes via the Favorite icon or from the object tab in the navigation menu. Let's look at both options.

Notes

The term "object" in Salesforce is referred to a module or table, for example, Account, Opportunity, Contact, Lead, Campaign, Case, etc. is an object. Each object stores every record as a row, and fields as columns, imagine the object like a big table with many rows and columns.

Accessing Favorites from Favorite icon

You can access your favorites from the Favorite icon, click the arrow next to the Favorite (star) icon, then click the item. Here, you will see a list of items that have been added as your Favorites, you need to scroll down if you have added a lot of items to your favorite list.

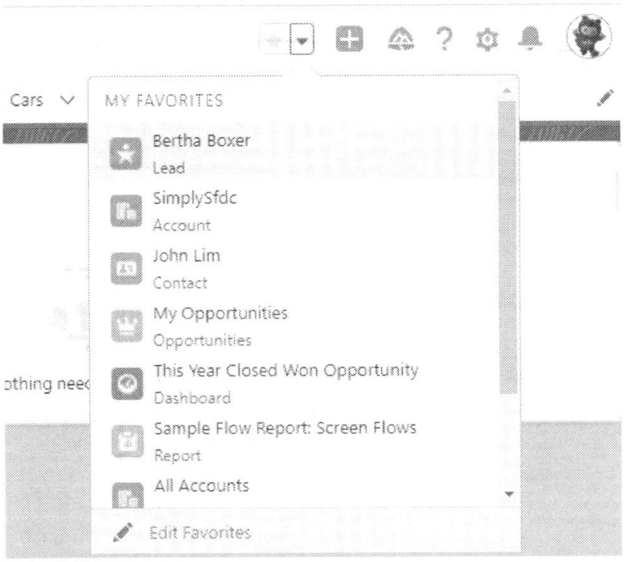

Figure 1.7 - Accessing existing Favorites

Tips

Make use of the **icon** before the record name or **label** below the favorite name to easily identify what kind of item is for each one. For example, *Bertha Boxer* is a lead, the icon will tell you that is a Lead record, and the **Lead** label shows under Bertha Boxer. The same applies to the Account, Contact, Report, etc. If the favorite item is a list view, the label would be in the plural form, such as Opportunities as in *Figure 1.7*.

Accessing Favorites from List View

Another place to access Favorites is via the object tab (e.g., Accounts, Leads, etc.) in the navigation menu. As we have added a Lead name Bertha Boxer as a favorite, let us use this Lead as an example:

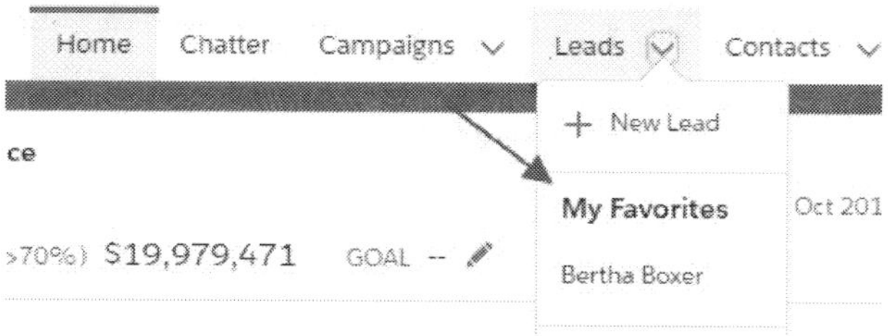

Figure 1.8 - Accessing favorite from an object in the tab

This is how we access our favorite lead record Bertha Boxer via the Leads tab:

1. Click the arrow next to the **Leads** tab
2. Notice below **+ New Lead**, there is a section called **My Favorites**. Underneath this, you will find all Leads that have been added as Favorites. Click the Lead to open it.

Personalizing the Navigation Bar

The navigation bar contains a set of tabs available for you to select, such as Home, Accounts, Leads, Report, etc. In the standard **Lightning Experience** user interface, all the tabs are shown horizontally, while in another user interface called **Lightning Console**, the tabs are shown vertically under the drop-down menu. Lightning Console was built for those needing to access multiple tabs at once, such as those in High-Velocity Sales or Service environments. If you need to change the navigation style from Lightning Experience to Lightning Console, or the other way round, reach out to your Salesforce admin or consultant.

This book will discuss the standard Lightning Experience only but personalizing the Lightning Console navigation bar is not very different. Below is a sample screenshot of Lightning Experience:

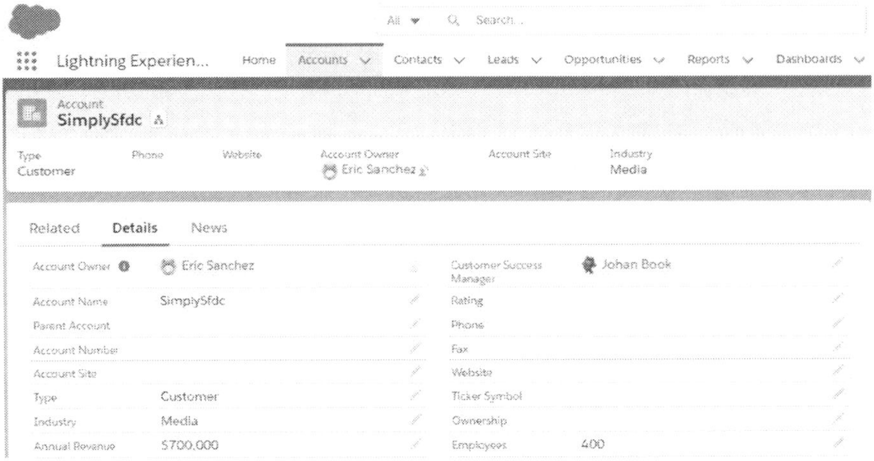

Figure 1.9 - Lightning Experience user interface

Alternatively, here is a sample of the Lightning Console user interface, where all menus are shown under a dropdown:

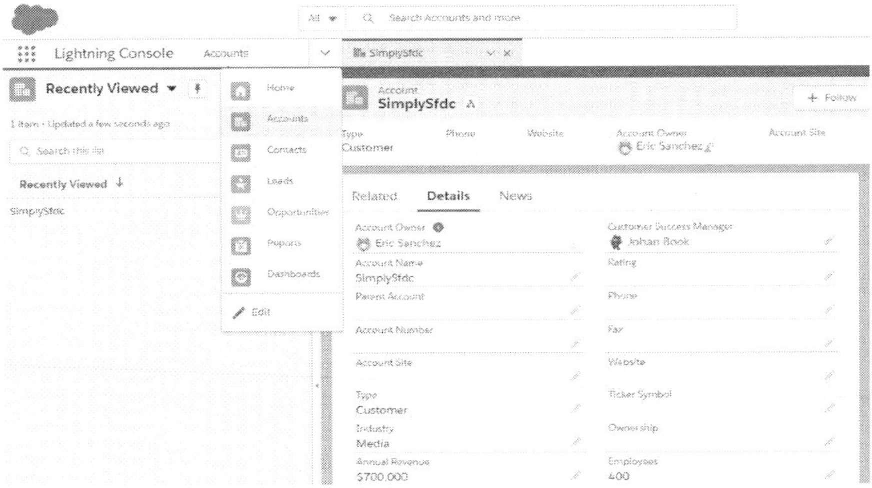

Figure 1.10 - Lightning Console user interface

When your Salesforce admin or consultant configures Salesforce for your company, they will add certain tabs that are used by most users, and the tabs will be set in a certain order.

The good news is, that the Salesforce platform allows us as a user to add and re-arrange the tabs order we prefer to work in. You can add tabs that are not visible by default, or even add a list view or a record as a tab. Since we work with the system daily, it is important to configure the user interface in a way that supports how we work.

Tips

To identify whether your app is enabled for Lightning Experience, look at the furthest right icon on the navigation bar. If you see a ***pencil*** icon, then the app is enabled for Lightning Experience. Otherwise, if you see an "i" (information) icon, then that is a Classic app, which does not support the personalization of the navigation bar. In that case, reach out to your Salesforce admin to enable and upgrade the app to Lightning Experience.

Rearranging tabs

You can easily re-arrange the order of tabs by dragging the tab and dropping it to your preferred location. For example, to move the Opportunities tab after the Home tab, simply drag and drop it as *Figure 1.9*:

Figure 1.11 - Re-ordering tabs

Ideally, you should move the more important tabs or most used tabs to the left (after the Home tab), then continue with the less important tabs. If you have too many tabs added to the navigation bar, they will be shown under the **More** tab, at the further right of the navigation bar.

Tips

The first four tabs from the left after the Home tab will be shown as the landing tabs in the Salesforce mobile app.

Adding tabs to the Navigation Bar

If you have tabs that do not appear in the navigation bar, such as Products, Asset, or a custom object, but you can access them from the 9-dots icon (at further left of the navigation bar) by typing the tab name, it would be more effective for you to add them as tabs in the navigation bar, if those tabs are frequently used.

Follow the steps below:

1. Click the pencil icon at the further right of the navigation bar

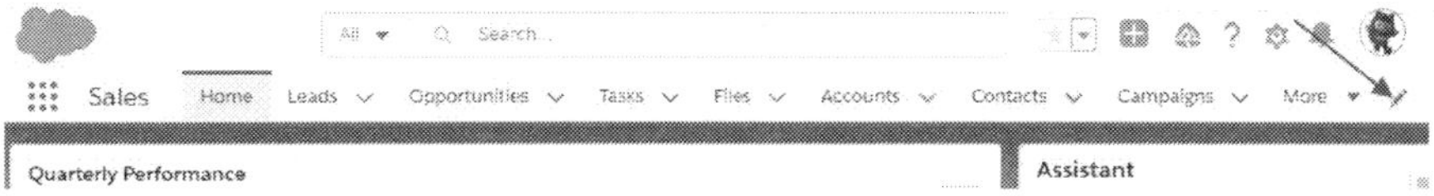

Figure 1.12 – Customize navigation bar

2. Click the **Add More Items** button:

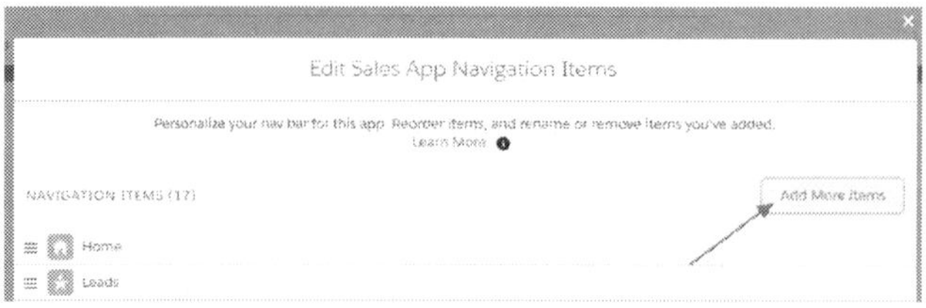

Figure 1.13 - Add More Items option

3. Click the **All** tab

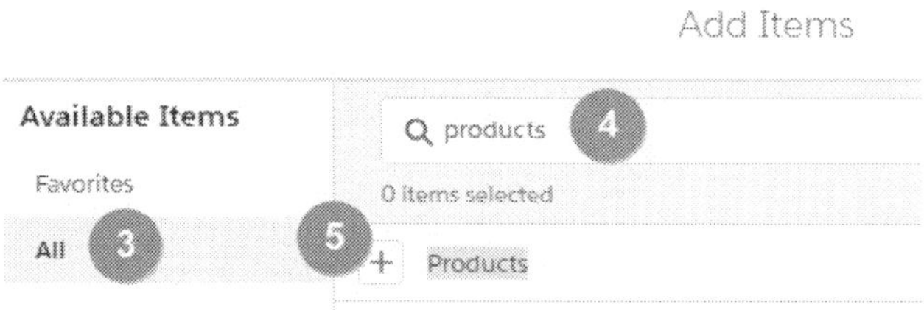

Figure 1.14 - Adding Items

4. Type the name of the tab you want to add to the search box. For this example, I am going to add Products as a tab, so I will type `products`.
5. Click the **+** icon next to Products, the icon will turn into a green checkmark once clicked.
6. Click **Add x Nav Item** button. If you just add one tab such as Products, x would be 1, so this depends on the number of tabs that you are adding.
7. Tabs will be added to the bottom in the app navigation items window:

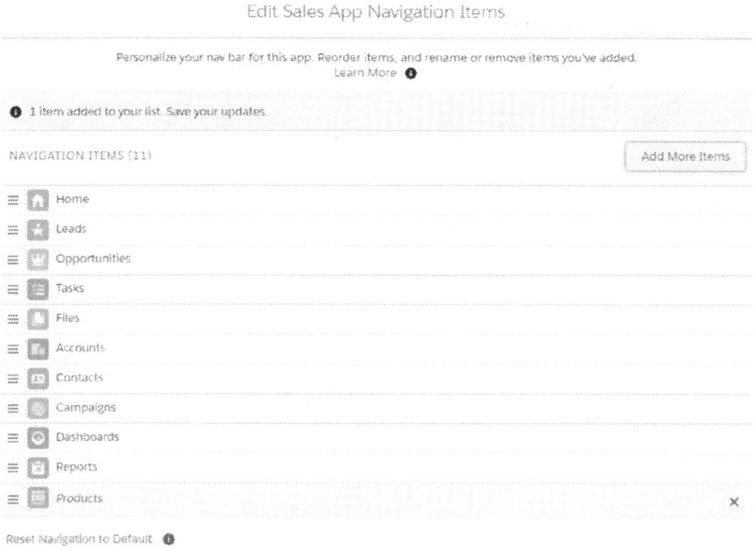

Figure 1.15 - Products added at the bottom of the navigation item

8. You can drag the tab to the upper level; the higher the tab, the further left it will be shown in the navigation bar. If you do not move this, it may fall under **More** if you have too many tabs that have been added.

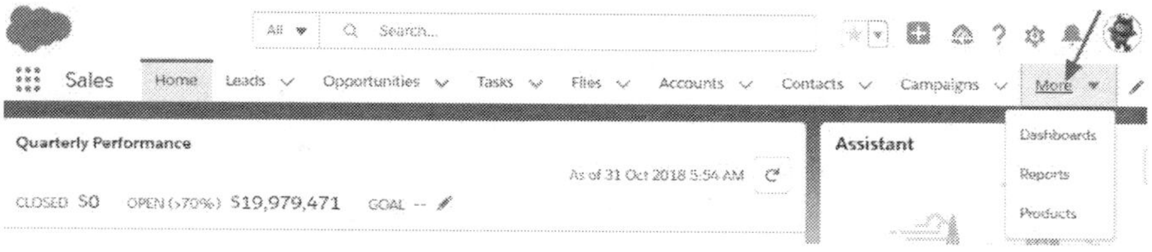

Figure 1.16 - Products added as the last item in the navigation bar

9. Click **Save** to save your changes.
10. In the above hands-on exercise, I dragged the Products tab just below the Opportunities tab, now I have the Products appear as a tab in the navigation menu before the Opportunities tab:

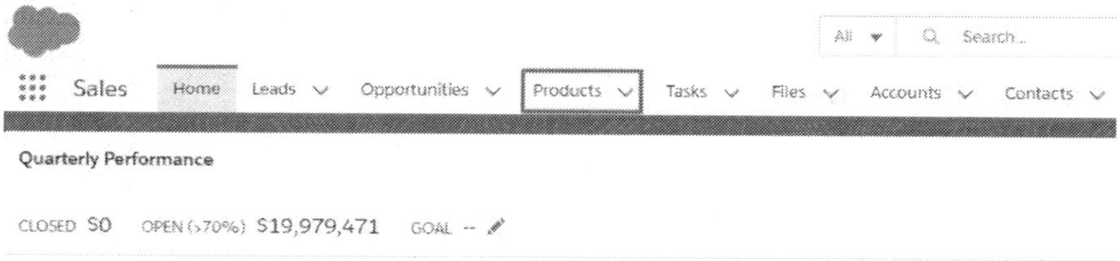

Figure 1.17 - The selected item added as a tab

The changes are just for you and don't impact any other users, and they will be there permanently until you remove them.

Adding tabs from Favorites

Similar to adding objects as a tab, items that have been added as Favorite can also be made as a tab. This means, you can add not just objects from the 9-dots icon, but also record, list view, etc. that are added as favorites can be added as a tab too. This is powerful, easy, and again does not impact any other users.

The steps are pretty similar to adding a tab from an object, such as when we added Products in the previous exercise. In this exercise, we are going to add 'Bertha Boxer' as a tab, Bertha Boxer is a Lead that has been added as a favorite.

1. Click the pencil icon at the far right of the navigation bar, as we did in the previous hands-on
2. Click the **Add More Items** button (again, seen in the previous hands-on challenge)
3. Look for `Bertha Boxer` in the Favorites tab (which is the default tab in this window)
4. Click + before the **Bertha Boxer** record name, the icon will turn into a green checkmark when selected

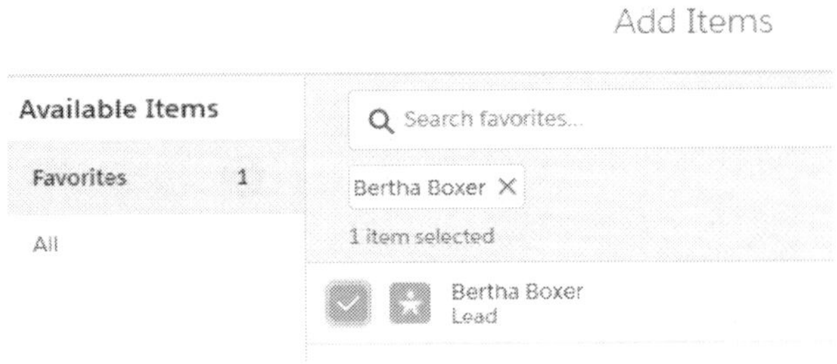

Figure 1.18 – Selecting the Favorites tab

5. Click **Add *x* Nav Item** button. Again, if you just add one tab such as Bertha Boxer, *x* would be *1*.
6. Tabs will be added at the bottom of the navigation items window. You can drag them to the upper level in the navigation item. The higher the tab, the further left it will be shown in the navigation bar.
7. Click the **Save** button to save the changes.

Similar to the Product tab added, now we have Bertha Boxer, which is a Lead, now appear as a tab on our personalized navigation bar:

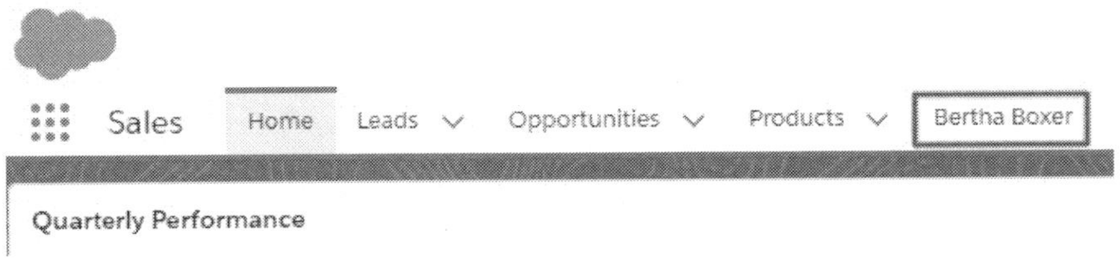

Figure 1.19 - A favorite record added as a tab

You can do the same by adding a report, dashboard, or List View as a tab too. For example, if you have a List View called `My Opportunities`, by adding the list view as a tab (make sure to add the list view as a Favorite first), you will be able to open the list view in **one click**:

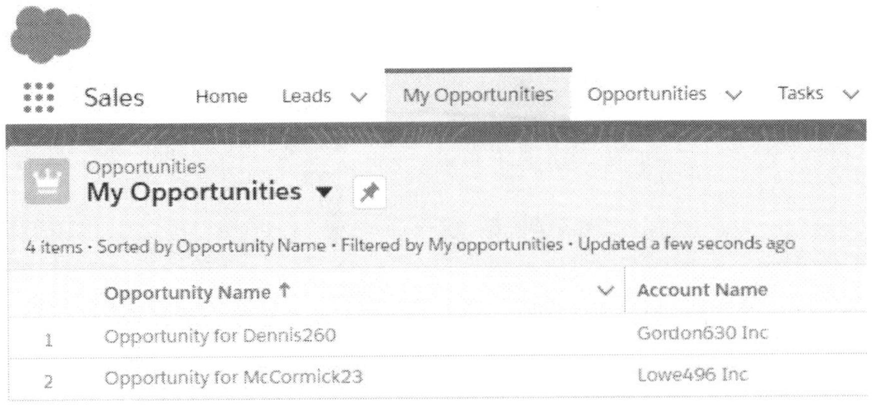

Figure 1.20 - My Opportunities list view added as a tab

Tips

You can rename tabs that have been added by clicking the pencil icon in the navigation bar, then click the pencil icon after the tab name, but you cannot rename tabs that have been added by default.

You can remove tabs that have been added manually, click the pencil icon in the navigation bar, then click the cross icon after the tab name, you also cannot remove tabs that have been added by default.

Pinning List View

When you click a tab, such as **Opportunity**, by default you will be landed at **Recently Viewed**. Recently Viewed is a list view which is a great feature that shows you all existing opportunities that you have opened recently in case you want to jump back to them.

However, in a certain part of your daily job, you need to monitor a particular list view, such as My Opportunities or My Cases. For example, by pinning the **My Opportunities** list view, every time you click the Opportunities tab, you will be landed at the **My Opportunities** list view, not the default Recently Viewed list view anymore.

This simple action will save you time in your day-to-day use of Salesforce. Imagine if you manually had to search and open the My Opportunity list view each time. A lot of time would be wasted doing that many times in a day.

We will learn more about the value and functionality of the list view in detail in *Chapter 2, The Power of List View*. For now, let's learn how to be more productive by pinning a list view of choice in a tab on our personalized navigation bar:

1. Click the **Opportunities** tab. You will see the Recently Viewed list view. This will look like so:

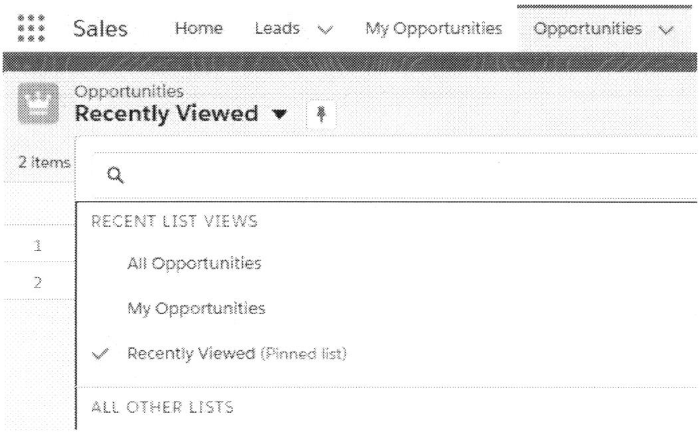

Figure 1.21 - Recently Viewed list view as Pinned list

2. Select **My Opportunities** list view

3. Click the **pin icon** to set the My Opportunities list view as the default list view

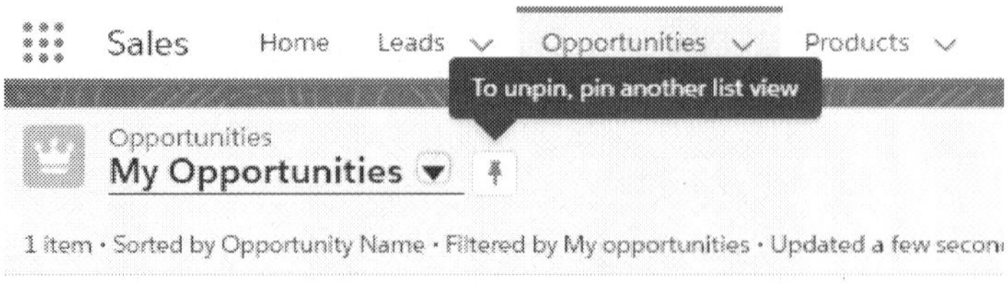

Figure 1.22 - My Opportunities list view as Pinned list

4. Click the **Home** tab, then click the **Opportunities** tab again. You will now see **My Opportunities**, instead of **Recently Viewed**.
5. To unpin, you need to pin another list view, which will become the default list view.

Best Practice

Depends on your job nature, if you need to keep monitor a list view, such as open cases, it makes sense to pin a list view, otherwise, keep the default Recently Viewed list view, with this you can easily open records recently viewed.

Personalizing Related List

You can personalize each object's related list, including reordering or hiding items. This change only applies to you, and Salesforce will remember your changes for future use. If you are unsure what a related list is, it is a child object, such as Opportunity related list on the Account page.

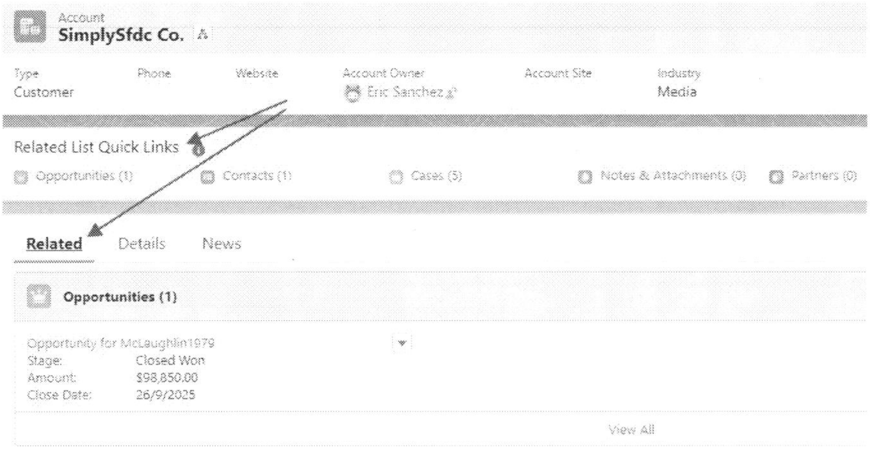

Figure 1.23 - Related list on the Account page

How to Personalize a Related List

Let's have a quick hands-on challenge to learn how to personalize the related list

1. Click your avatar at the upper right corner of the Lightning page
2. Click **Settings**, then click > **Display & Layout** then **Customize My Pages**
3. Select an object that you want to change, in this sample, I am going to move Contacts above Opportunities in the Account page, so select **Account**, then click **Customize Page** button

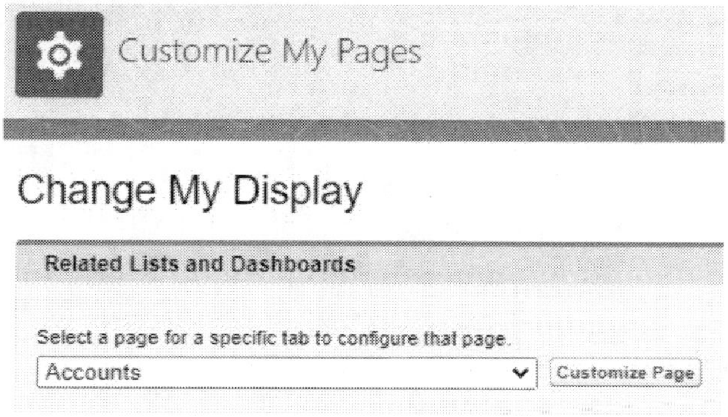

Figure 1.24 - Customize related list on the Account

4. Move **Contacts** to the top. If you want to hide an item, select the object, and click **Remove**, in this hands-on challenge, I am going to remove **Cases**.

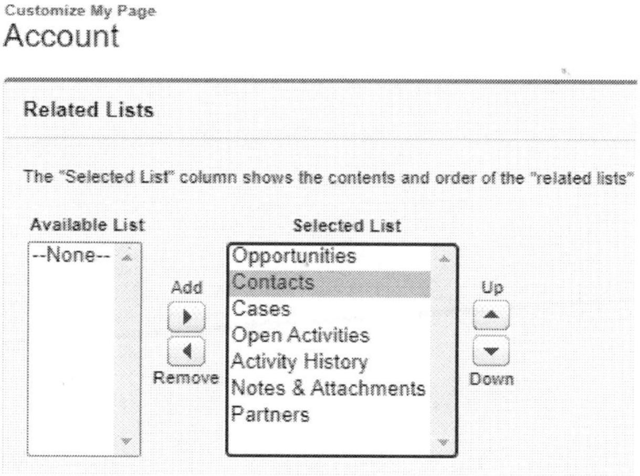

Figure 1.25 - Selecting related list for the Account page

5. Click the **Save** button and done.

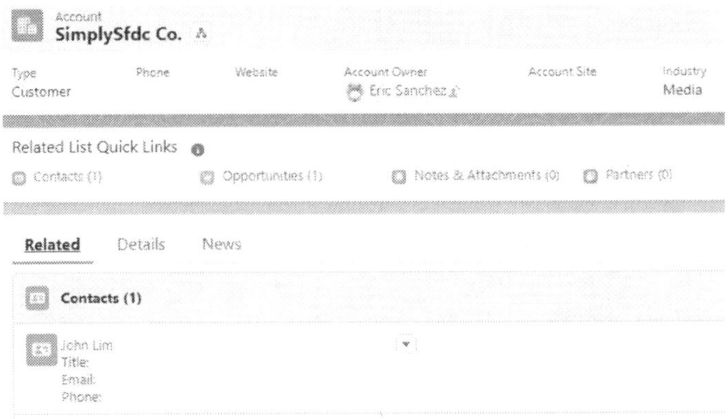

Figure 1.26 - Customize related list on the Account

In *Figure 1.26*, **Contacts** moves the furthest left in the **Related List Quick Links** component and at the top of the Related tab, also the Cases related list is no longer show.

> **Best Practice**
>
> By personalizing the related list, such as hiding certain tabs, you will miss information related to a record, so make sure that you do not need that info before hiding the tab. Reordering tabs will not impact your visibility, but if your role is to support and deal with a lot of users, it is good to keep the default order.

Summary

In this chapter, we have learned a lot of items that we can customize in the Lightning Experience user interface. Here are items to follow as best practice:

- Always set display density that works better for yourself, some people prefer Compact, and some prefer Comfy, there is nothing wrong or right here.
- Make use of the favorite feature to make your life easier when working in Salesforce:
    - » Only add to favorite for something you need to work often, such as a report
    - » Only add records to favorite that you need to follow-up
    - » Remove items from favorite once no longer needed
    - » Remember that you also can access favorites from the tabs and mobile app
- Personalize your navigation bar
    - » Moving the more important tabs at the left side of the navigation bar
    - » Add tabs, list view, or record that mostly use as tabs in your navigation bar

- When clicking a tab, instead of opening the default Recently Viewed, you can change this behavior by pinning to another list view, for example, if you spend more time or need to monitor records in that list view.
- Make use of the personalized related list, move the most important objects for you at the top, and hide the one that is not relevant at all for you.

CHAPTER 2:

THE POWER OF LIST VIEW

In this chapter, we will learn about **List View** in-depth, focusing on its power and benefits, such as mass action and mass update, as well as why and when we should and should not use a List View.

Here are the main topics that we will go through in this chapter:

- Introducing List View
- Creating and editing List View
- Types of List View
- Performing mass actions and mass updates in List View
- Adding charts to List View

By end of this chapter, you will master creating, editing, and sharing List View with your team, as well as knowing each type of List View, and the best practices for using them.

Introducing List View

If you have used Salesforce for some time, you probably already use List View without knowing it. List View provides a list of records of an object in Salesforce based on the defined filters, and this can be in a table or Kanban format. The object we speak of here refers to Account, Opportunity, Case, etc.

When you click a tab in Salesforce such as the Accounts tab, you will land on a list view. By default, it will be the Recently Viewed list view, but we can change this to another list view by pinning it, as we learned in *Chapter 1, Customizing My User Interface.*

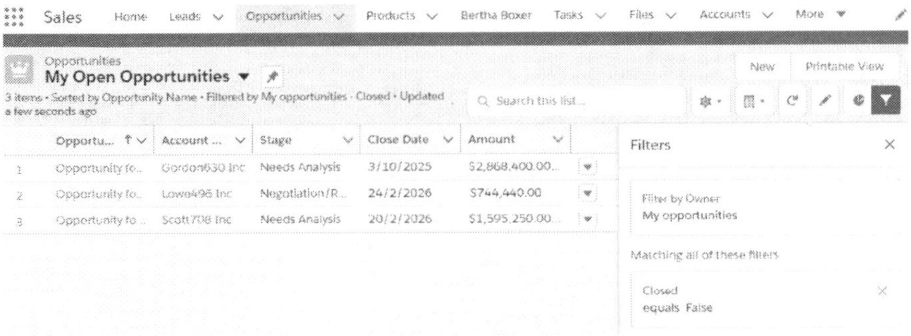

Figure 2.1 – Sample of a list view

List View ideally is used to show or monitor open items only, such as Open Opportunities, My Team Open Cases, etc., whether the Opportunities or Cases are unassigned, owned by you or your team members.

The key word here is open as in an open status, but can you also use a List View to show all data or a group of data? Yes, the system will not stop you, but that is not recommended nor best practice. Instead, you should use a report for that purpose, because:

- List View only initially shows up to 50 records on a page. To sees more data, you need to keep scrolling down.
- There is a maximum of 15 columns (or fields) exposed in a List View
- You cannot export data from a List View
- You cannot use fields from the parent object to the list view or use it as a list view filter, e.g., an Opportunity List View cannot use Account fields. You can ask your Salesforce admin to create formula fields, but that is not practical.

All the above limitations do not exist when using reports. Let us see the comparison between List View and Report in the following table:

	List View	**Report**
Filters	Open items	As required
Mass action	Yes	No
Mass update	Yes	No
Export data and Subscribe to email	No	Yes
Group data	No	Yes
Cross filter, bucketing, and formula	No	Yes
Refer to field from parent object	No	Yes
Store in Folder and Subfolder	No	Yes
Display Type	List, Kanban, Split	Tabular, Summary, Matrix, Joined

Table 2.1 – View versus report

As you can see from the table, both List View and Reports have their benefits, so make sure to use the right tool for the right purpose.

Best Practice

Use List View only for open items and use reports for the rest.

Creating and Editing List Views

Creating a List View is simple. As an example, let's create My Open Opportunities list view:

1. Click the Opportunities tab so you land on the List View
2. Click the gear icon (1) at the upper right corner next to search the list search box
3. Click New (2) from list view controls

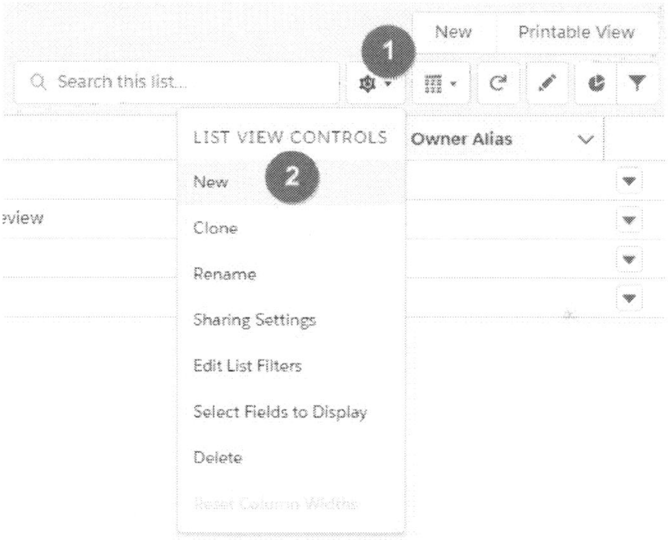

Figure 2.2 – List view controls

Note

If you do not see New option under list view control as in *Figure 2.2*, reach out to your Salesforce admin to grant you Create and Customize List Views permission.

4. For the List Name, type My Open Opportunities

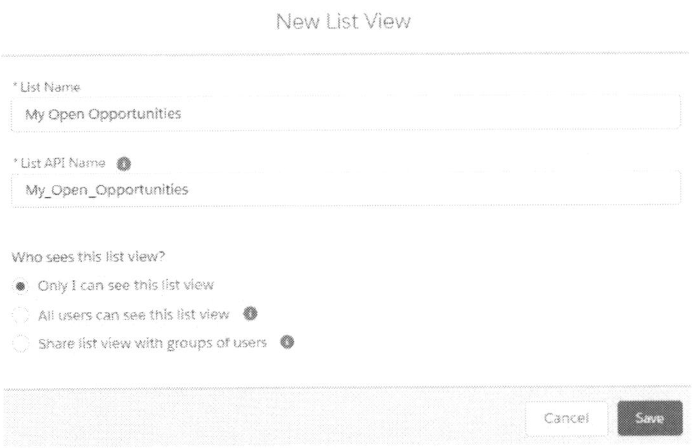

Figure 2.3 – creating a new list view

5. List API Name will be auto populated, then click the Save button. By default, you can create list views that only you can view and manage. Further permission may allow you to create List Views to be shared – see below for more information on this.
6. By default, the newly created list view will filter the owner by My Opportunities, since we would like to show only open Opportunities for this list view, click the Add Filter (3) link
7. Select Field "Closed" (4) equals False (5) which exposes every opportunity in an open pipeline stage (not Closed Lost or Closed Won), and then click the Done button (6)

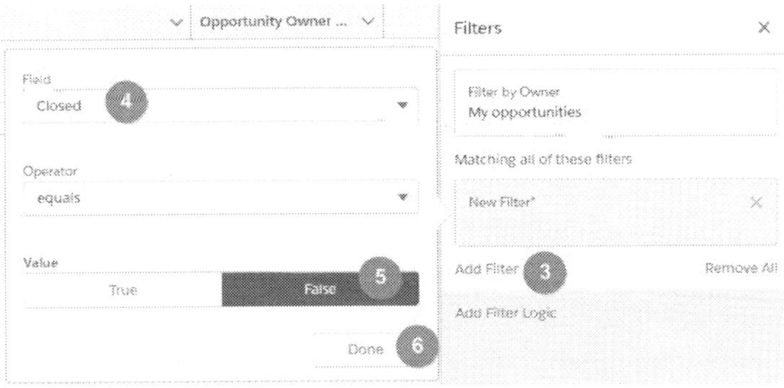

Figure 2.4 – Adding a filter to list view

8. Click the Save button.

You have just successfully created a new List View. Below is a sample in *Figure 2.5*, you will see a different list of Opportunities because your data is different from mine.

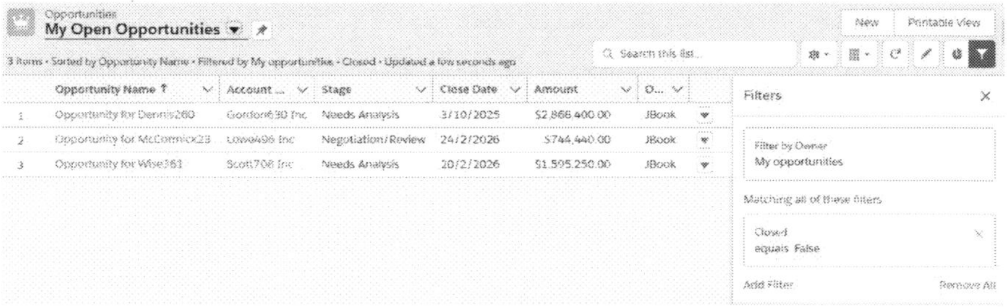

Figure 2.5 – My Open Opportunities list view

The List View created in *Figure 2.5* will have a few default fields automatically added, such as Opportunity Name, Account Name, and so on. Now, let us modify the List View created by adding and removing fields as needed:

9. Open the List View created, by selecting it from the dropdown menu or simply type in the List View name.

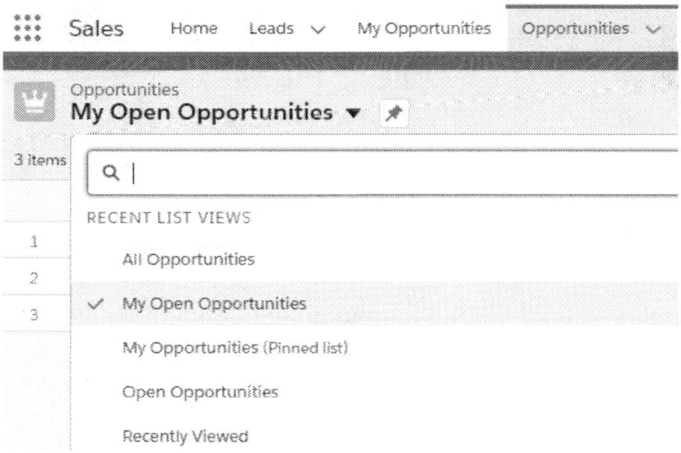

Figure 2.6 – Open list view created

10. Click the gear icon as shown in *Figure 2.2*
11. Click Select Fields to Display
12. Remove Opportunity Owner Alias from the Visible Fields box and add Owner Full Name from the Available Fields box by clicking the small arrows between the two Available and Visible Fields boxes. Use the far right up/down arrows to sort the field/column order.
13. Click the Save button.

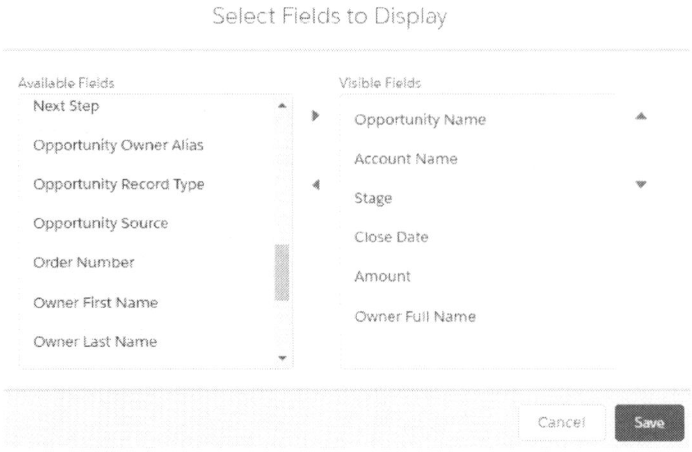

Figure 2.7 – Adding and removing fields from a list view

Now that the List View is updated with new fields, you can play around with the view, for example, by changing the sort field by clicking the field header for ascending and then clicking it again to sort by descending view. You also can change the field/column width by dragging the line between the field names.

> **Tips**
>
> If you have more than 1 filter on the list view, you can add Filter Logic. By default, the relation between all filters is AND, using filter logic, you can use AND, OR, and () to set order of precedence, for example, if you have 4 filters added, you can set filter logic such as 1 AND 2 AND (3 OR 4).

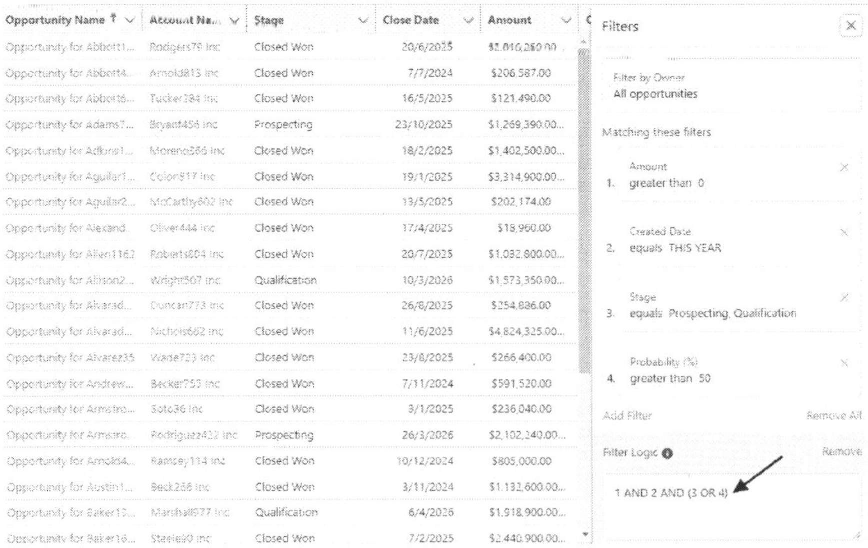

Figure 2.8 – A List View with Filter Logic

Sharing List View

So, you have completed a hands-on exercise of creating and editing a List View, but that view is only visible to you. You need to share it with your team members, so everyone in the team will see the filtered data using the same list view. So, how can you share a list view?

Refer to *Figure 2.3*, at the bottom of that window, you will see the option Who sees this list view? When you create a new List View, if it is intended to be shared with your team or everyone in the company, you should select options (b) and (c) as below:

1. Only I can see this List View – this is the default option
2. All users can see this List View – this will allow all users that have access to Salesforce able to see the List View created
3. Share List View with groups of users – this option allows you to share the List View to users in Public Group or users with specific Roles

Tips and Note

If you are unable to select (b) and (c) in Who sees this list view? reach out to your Salesforce admin to grant you Manage Public List Views permission.

The power to share a List View comes with the responsibility that if you edit or delete it, all users will see the new version or will no longer be able to access it.

However, if the List View has been created and only you can see it, to share or edit the sharing access, click the gear icon as in *Figure 2.2* then select Sharing Settings.

Best Practice

Before you delete or update a list view, always make sure that you are deleting or updating the right list view. Once it is deleted or updated, it will be permanently removed or updated with the changes, you can only manually revert by re-creating or update the list view if you have a screenshot served as backup or copy from a sandbox.

Other actions in List View controls

As demonstrated in *Figure 2.2*, you can also perform the following actions in a List View, but this is not applicable for the out of the box Recently Viewed list:

- **Clone** – to clone the currently opened list to a new List View
- **Rename** – to rename the List View
- **Sharing Settings** – to change visibility as discussed in the previous section
- **Edit List Views** – to edit the filters

- **Select Fields to Display** – to update fields showing, to a maximum of 15 columns
- **Delete** – to delete the currently opened List View.

By now, you will have mastered creating, editing, and sharing List Views with your team. You also learned that you could clone, rename, and filter List View data too.

> **Best Practices**
>
> Make sure the name of your List View name is clear and represents its intended purpose e.g., My Open Opportunities.
>
> Avoid creating a similar or duplicate name of List Views, only add fields required for that List View and try to refrain from adding too many columns.
>
> Share the List View only to the users that need it. If it is created only for your personal use, do not share it.

Types of List View

When you create a List View or open one created by your team, it will be displayed in a Table format as we saw in *Figure 2.1*, where each field is displayed as a column. In addition to the Table view, Salesforce also offers two more views: **Kanban** view and **Split** view. Let's explore each of these in this section. Since we have covered the **Table** view in the previous section in this chapter, so we will not discuss it again here.

Kanban View

Kanban view is useful if you want to group data, such as by Stage or Status or other fields as needed. Additionally, you can also summarize data in this view, for example, if you want to get the total of Opportunity Amount within a Stage in the List View.

To change from Table view to Kanban view, simply click the icon next to the gear icon, then select **Kanban**.

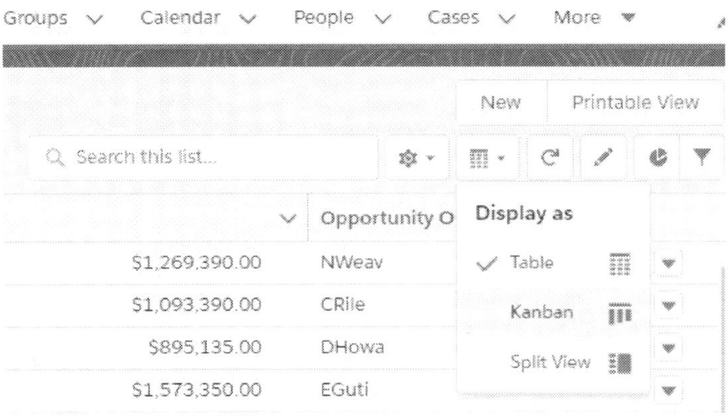

Figure 2.9 – To change list view display

Depending on the object, the first time you select Kanban for a List View, the system will ask for the Kanban setting:

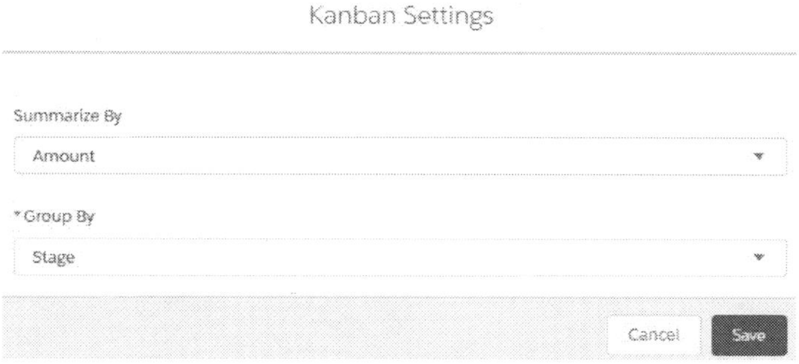

Figure 2.10 – Select field for Kanban Setting

There are two items in the Kanban settings:

- **Summarize By** (this is not mandatory), example: to Summarize by Amount
- **Group By** (this is mandatory), example: Group by Opportunity Stage

Kanban View will show each record as a card with a maximum of 4 fields, these 4 fields are the first 4 fields selected in the Table view. You cannot do sorting in Kanban View, but it will be based on sorting in the Table view. You can open the record or select other actions from the dropdown arrow menu, such as Edit, Delete, or Change Owner (depending on permissions that you have on the record).

Kanban View allows you to move the data by drag and drop across the column to update the data. This view is great for easily updating on status, such as moving the stage of an Opportunity from Prospecting to Qualification, see *Figure 2.11*. To moves an Opportunity Stage in Kanban, you can simply drag the opportunity record's box across from the **Prospecting** to **Qualification** column.

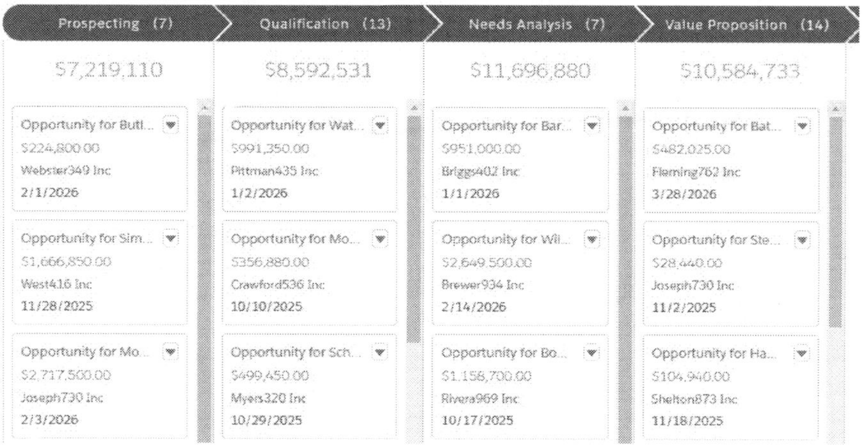

Figure 2.11 – List view display as Kanban

Salesforce will remember the type of view selected when you last opened the List View and stick with that. For example, if you opened the List View as Kanban, opening the same list again will leave the display as Kanban view. When you select Kanban view, click the gear icon and you will see **Kanban Settings** at the last option, where you can change the field for grouping and summarize by, as shown in *Figure 2.10.*

Split View

Split View will split the screen into 2 panels: the **left panel** as a List View with the list of data, and the **right panel** to show the record layout and the record detail, based on the selected record at the left panel. This view is useful when you need to flip through a list of records without going back and forth between views. Same as Kanban view, only a maximum of 4 fields will be displayed in the List View, and these 4 fields are the first 4 fields in the Table view order. You cannot sort by a field in Split View, but it will be based on sorting done in the Table view.

You can hide the left panel by clicking the arrow on the separation bar for a bigger screen on the record detail. Click the same arrow again to open the List View panel:

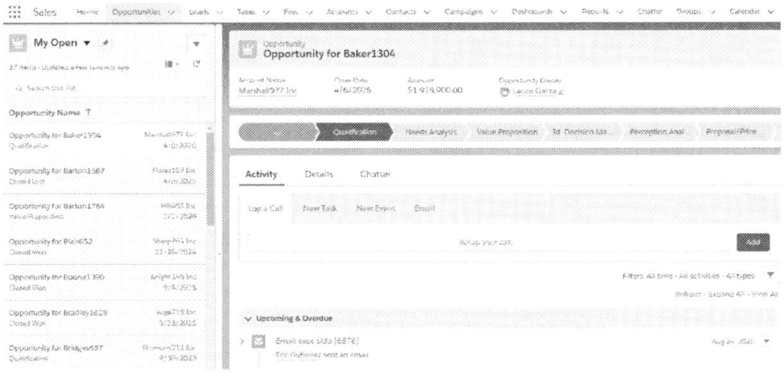

Figure 2.12 – List view displayed as Split View

We have now learned about the different views available to you in a List View and the benefits of each. You can always change the view as needed whilst working.

Performing Mass Actions with List View

One of the most powerful features of using List Views is the **mass action capability** -- performing an action on multiple records, and **mass update** -- carrying out inline editing across multiple records. We will focus on both of these in this and the next section.

Firstly, do you notice that each tab offers different List View buttons by default? For example, Lead and Contact have a **Send List View** button, whilst the Case tab has a **Change Owner** button? Your Salesforce admin would have created additional buttons as per your company needs. These buttons offer you the capability to perform mass actions across multiple records, such as mass change the Case owner on all Cases that you select.

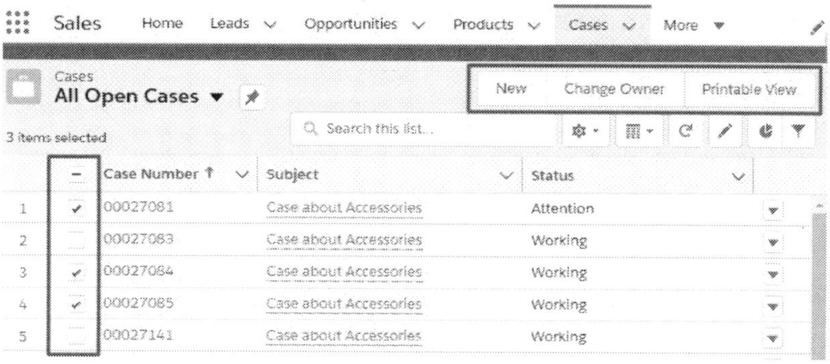

Figure 2.13 – Buttons of Case list view

As you see in *Figure 2.13*, we can select multiple records, then click a button to act on the records selected.

> **Note**
>
> Not all buttons in the List View will perform mass action, for example, if you select multiple cases then click the New button, then the selected cases will be ignored.

Next, let get hands-on and do a mass owner update in a Case List View.

Hands-on Exercise: Mass Change Owner

In this exercise, we will mass assign all open cases to a team member. We will start by creating a custom List View called **Unassigned Cases**. In this example: the unassigned Cases mean that Cases are still owned by a queue, for my example, I have a queue called **APAC Regional Support**.

1. Click **Cases** tab (1)
2. Click **gear icon** (2) then click **New** (3)

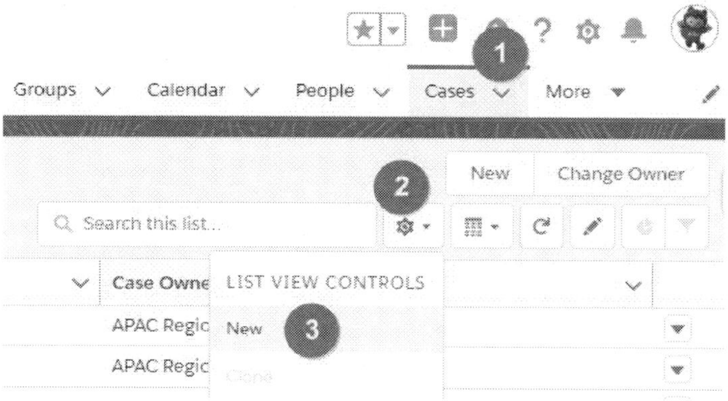

Figure 2.14 – Create new list view on Case

3. For the **List Name** textbox, type `Unassigned Cases` (4) then click the **Save** button (5)

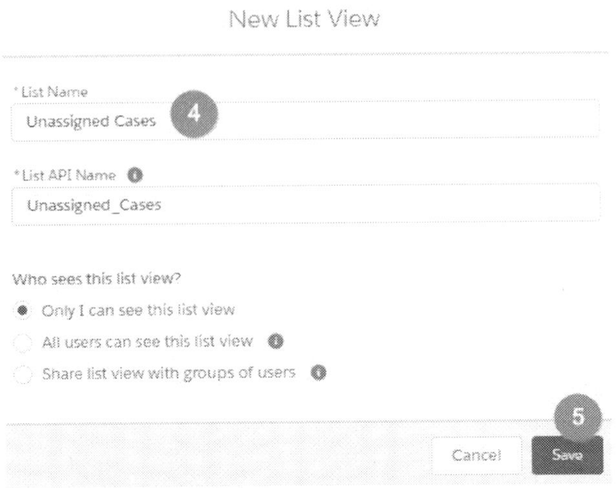

Figure 2.15 – Enter list view name

4. Change **Filter by Owner** to **All cases** (6), then add filter **Owner Name** = `APAC Regional Support` (7) then click the **Save** button (8).

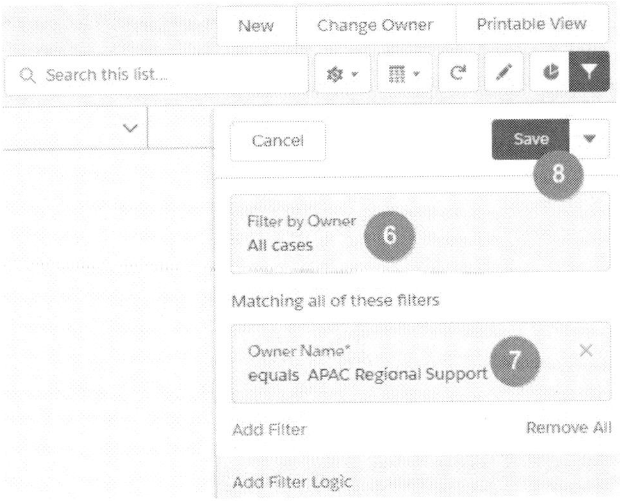

Figure 2.16 – Enter list view name

5. Next, we are going to select fields to be displayed in this List View. Click the **gear icon** again (9), then **Select Fields to Display** (10).

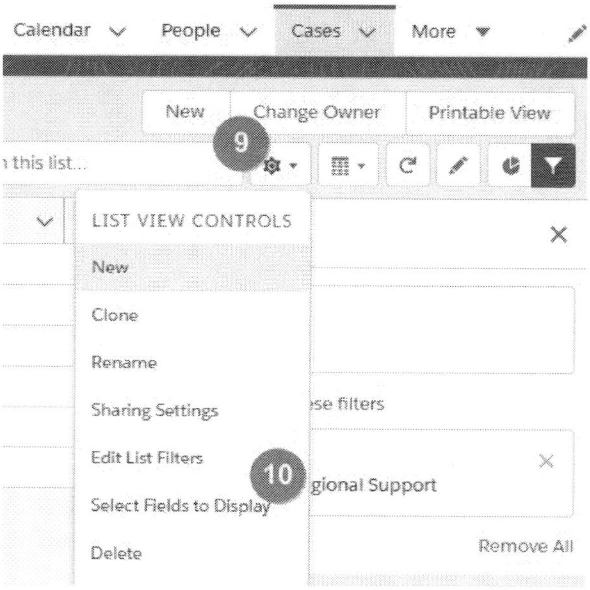

Figure 2.17 – Select Fields to Display

6. Let's select the following fields:
7. Case Number
8. Subject
9. Status
10. Owner Name
11. Click the **Save** button, up until here, we have created a new List View with all Cases that still own by the APAC Regional Support queue.

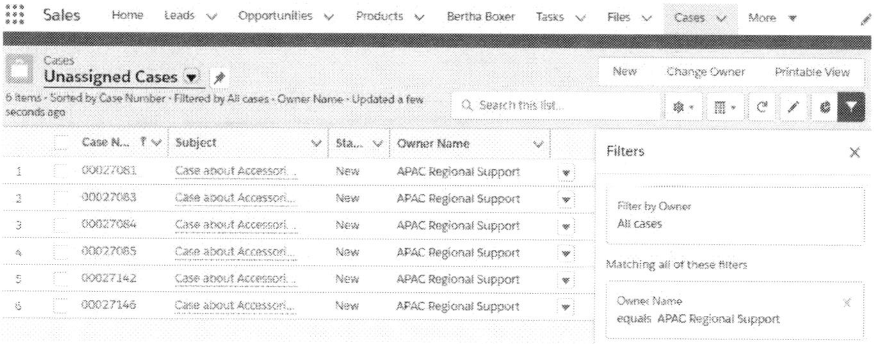

Figure 2.18 – Unassigned Case list view

12. Select a few Cases by selecting in the 1st column checkbox (11), then click the **Change Owner** (12) button. Type in a *user name* to be assigned for selected Cases (13), then click **Submit** button (14).

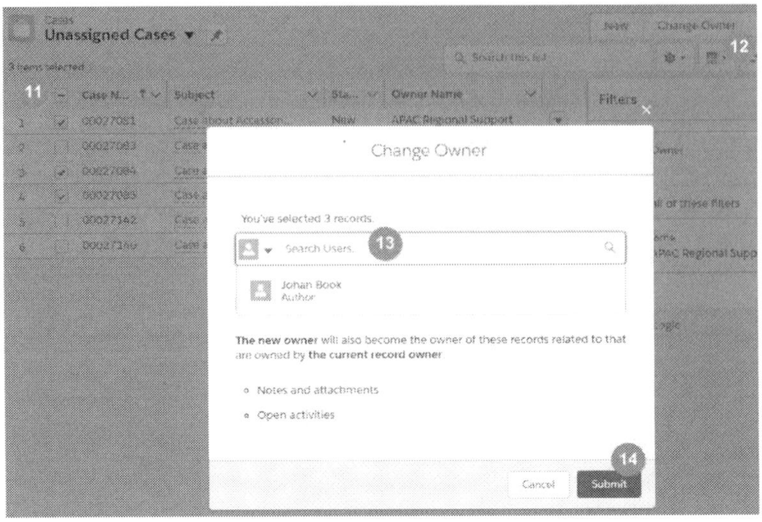

Figure 2.19 – Mass change owner for selected cases

13. The selected Cases have been assigned to a user, and they no longer show in the `Unassigned Cases` List View.

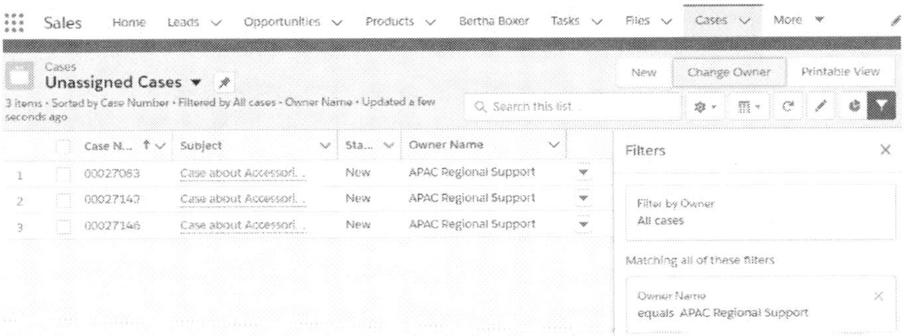

Figure 2.20 – The remaining unassigned cases

To mass assign Cases to a different user, repeat step 8 by selecting the remaining Cases.

Performing Mass Update with List View

Another powerful feature offers by List View is the ability to mass update the value of a column across many records in a List View. For example, we would like to mass update the Status for a few selected Cases.

1. Open the Case List View and make sure the **Status** field is added.
2. Select the Cases where Status needs to be updated (1).
3. Hover your mouse over the Status column on any of the selected Cases (2). You should see a **pencil icon** at the end of the Status cell, which you should click

Figure 2.21 – Select cases for inline editing from a list view

4. Now you will see all the available Statuses. Select a new Status - I selected **Escalated** for this hands-on exercise. Now select the checkbox to update the selected items (3), then click **Apply** button (4)

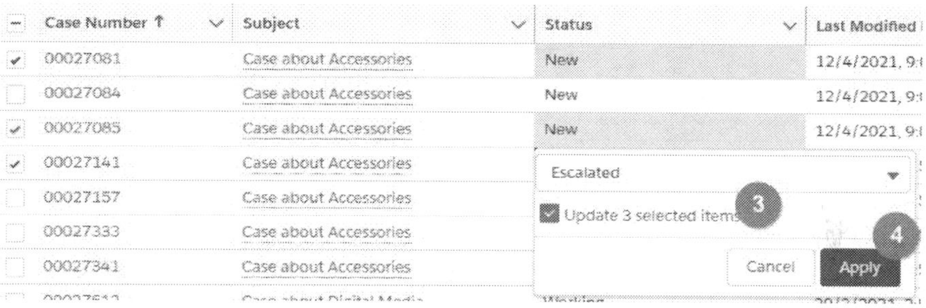

Figure 2.22 – Select new status for the selected cases

5. Click the **Save** button (5) at the bottom of the screen to confirm your changes

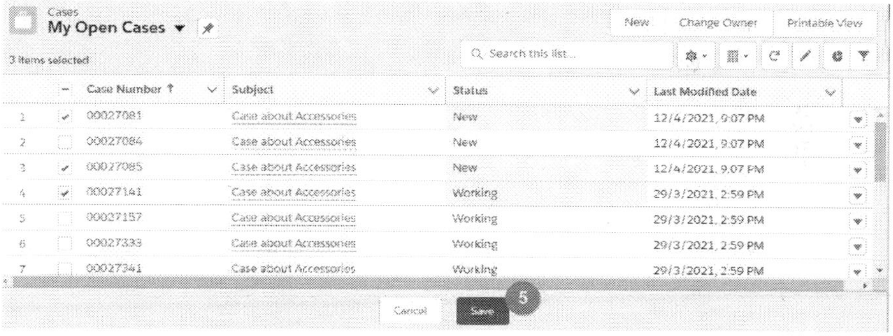

Figure 2.23 – Applying change for selected cases

6. You will see the Status of all selected Cases is updated with the new value of **Escalated**.

Figure 2.24 – Status for selected Cases is updated

Tips

If the object is configured with more than one **Record Type**, in order to do inline editing, the List View must have **Record Type** added as a **filter** and contain only **one value**. Additionally, not all fields can be updated using inline editing, such as Owner Name. If the field is unable to be edited in the List View, it will show a lock icon on the far right of the field instead of a pencil icon.

In this section, we learned how you can perform mass action and mass update on a List View, instead of changing the data one by one by opening each record. These 'short-cuts' will save you a lot of time in your daily job.

Adding Charts to List View

We also can add charts into a List View. This is very useful for you to get a summary of the data at a glance, and without going through each record individually. For example, you can see the percentage of open Opportunities by Stage, or how many Cases have yet to be assigned.

To add a chart, group your data based on a field, for example, to see the number of open Cases by Status. In this example, I have a Case List View with a filter **Closed** equals **False**.

1. Open a List View, then click the **Chart** icon before the Filter icon.
2. Depending on the Object type there may be defaults. For example, Opportunity by default will be group by Stage, Case by default will be group by Status, etc. For a custom Object, if the List View does not have a chart added yet, click the **New Chart** button.
3. Enter the `Chart Name`, select a **Chart Type**, **Aggregate Type**, **Aggregate Field**, and **Grouping Field**. Then click the **Save** button.

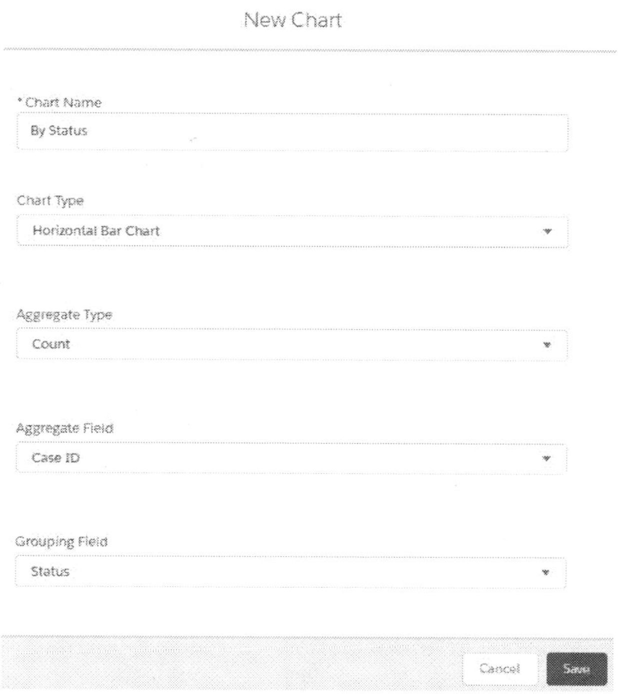

Figure 2.25 – Adding a chart to List View

4. Now that we have a chart added to the List View, notice that Chart icon (1) is selected. You can change the chart type by clicking the gear icon (2) below the chart.

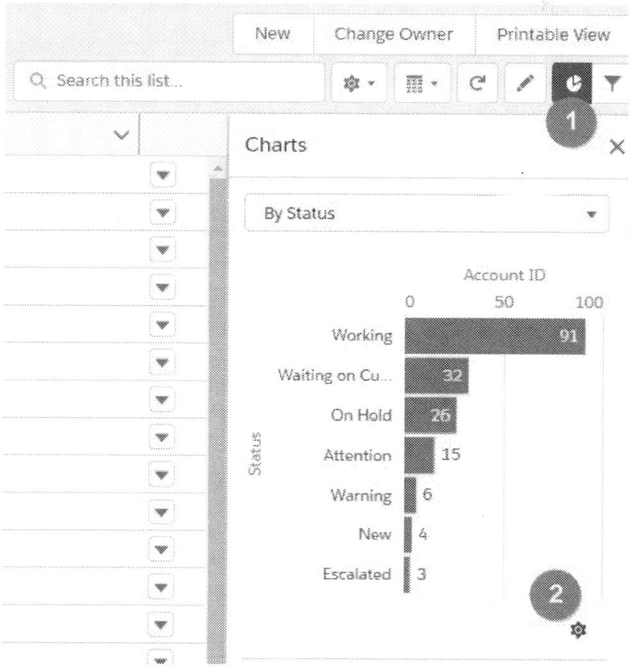

Figure 2.26 – Chart in List View

5. You have options to display the chart as:
6. Vertical Bar Chart, or
7. Horizontal Bar Chart, or
8. Donut Chart

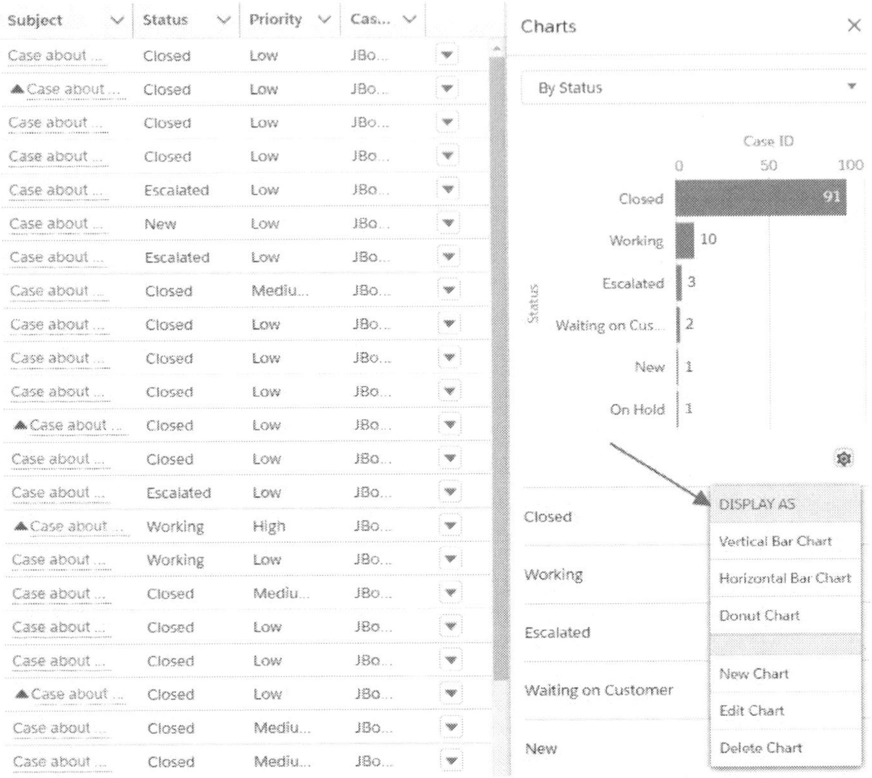

Figure 2.27 – Options for your Chart by clicking the Gear icon below the chart

9. As in *Figure 2.27*, you also have options to:
10. Add new Chart
11. Edit existing Chart
12. Delete existing Chart
13. We can have multiple charts in a List View. Let's add another chart by clicking **New Chart** from the gear icon, enter the `Chart Name`, select the **Chart Type**, **Aggregate Type**, **Aggregate Field**, and **Grouping Field**, for this hands-on exercise, select **Account Name,** refer to *Figure 2.28*.

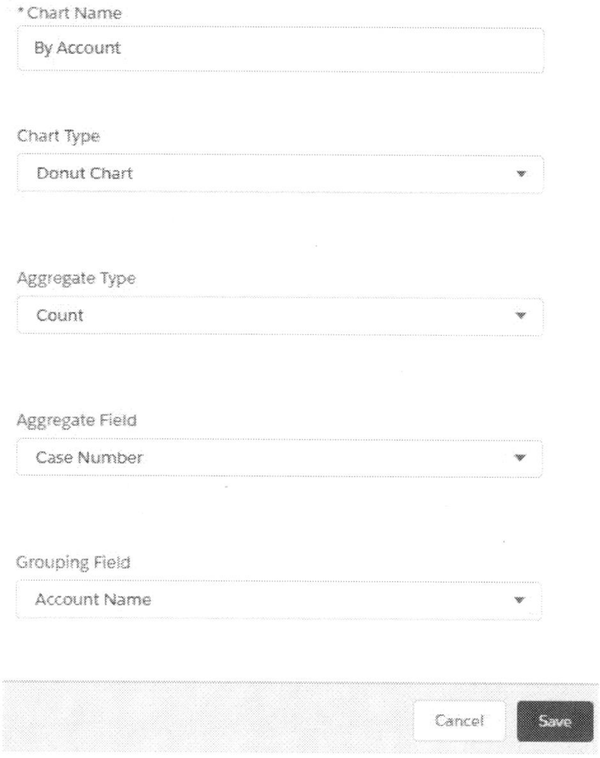

Figure 2.28 – Having multiple Charts in a List View

14. Once added, we can select to display which chart by selecting Chart Name in the dropdown menu.

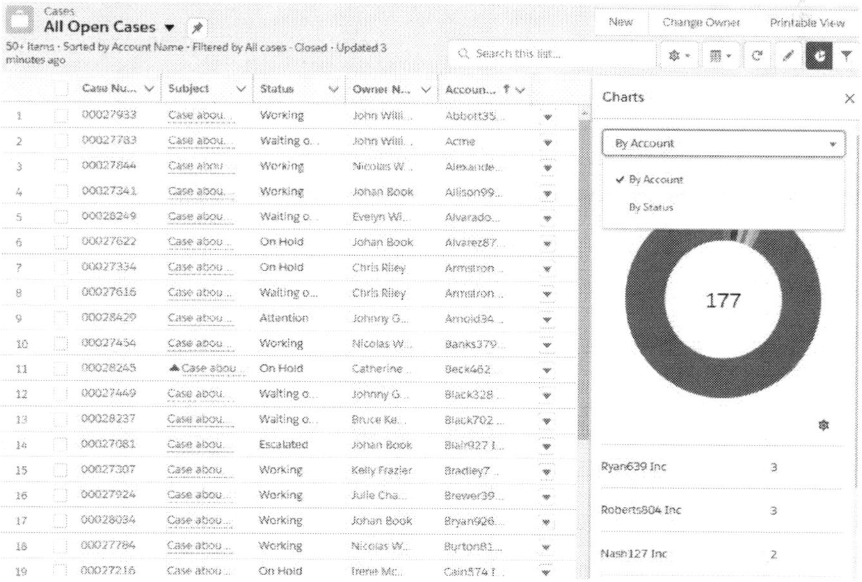

Figure 2.29 – Selecting a chart in a list view

Now you know how to add a chart in a List View, and you can add multiple charts for different purposes, such as one grouped by Status, and the other one grouped by Owner.

Summary

In this chapter, we explored in-depth the capabilities of the List View. Here are a few best practices:

- When creating a List View, always filter for open items only. For objects without a status, e.g., Account or Contact, leave the List View pinned to the default Recently Viewed view.
- List View has record limits and therefore is not the right tool to see a lot of data. Instead, use the reports tool for this purpose.
- Although the List View allows you to have up to 15 fields added, the columns will become very narrow, so only add the necessary fields.
- Create List Views that are shared with the team, so all team members see the same data.
- Make use of mass action, such as to change Owner or change Status for multiple records.
- Make use of mass inline edit to update multiple records without opening the individual records. You need to add a filter for Record Type if multiple Record Types are configured for that object.
- Add charts to the List View to see snapshots of the data at a glance.

Once you implement all the best practices discussed in this chapter, such as only using List View for the right use cases, sharing List Views with your team, and performing mass actions and mass edits, you should be much more productive working in Salesforce.

CHAPTER 3:

COLLABORATE WITH CHATTER

In this chapter, we will discuss Salesforce's **collaboration** tool. Collaboration is the key to success. If you are a sales rep, you may need to reach out to your sales support, legal, or product department, etc. to help you close a deal. You could send emails to many teams; however, your email may be lost in the many received by those users and may get buried down in their inbox, making it harder to find over time.

Salesforce's collaboration tool, **Chatter** offers your solution. Chatter is part of the Salesforce platform, which means you can use it without additional cost or licenses. With Chatter, you can directly collaborate with your team members in Salesforce right from a record page or a Group.

Chatter also allows you to follow people and records that you are interested in, for example, you may want to get updated for changes on a big opportunity owned by one of your reps. Furthermore, you also can set the frequency on how often you get email notifications from Chatter.

Here are the main topics that we will go through in this chapter:

- How to access Chatter
- Personalizing Chatter Notifications
- Using Chatter on your Profile page
- Following Users and Records with Chatter
- Working in the Chatter tab
- Using Chatter Groups and Chatter Streams
- Record Feeds

Personalizing Chatter Notifications

Similar to social media, Chatter can send you an email notification based on other users' interactivity with you in Chatter, or for people and records that you follow. For example, to alert you that someone started following you, mentioned your name, commented on your post, changes to a record you follow, and for many more reasons. You can also select to receive a daily or weekly digest for posts and interactions on your personal feed and Groups.

Chatter offers great flexibility for you to personalize your Chatter email notifications. You can configure the following items

1. Do you want to receive email notifications at all?
2. If you want to receive emails (see point 1), how frequently do you want to be notified?
3. If you want to receive emails (see point 1), what type of notifications, and from which Chatter Group?

Setting up Chatter Notifications

Chatter notifications are set in your personal settings, so whatever you change here will not impact other users. You can set up your Chatter notification from here:

1. Click your avatar from the upper right corner of the Lightning page
2. Click **Settings** under your name
3. Under the **Chatter** tab, click **Email Notifications**
4. Select or deselect all items as your preference
5. Click **Save**

Figure 3.1 – Chatter Email Notifications Settings

In the **Chatter Email Settings**, the first question is, do you want to receive emails notification from Chatter? If you unselect the **Receive emails** checkbox, then nothing else needs to be configured and you will not receive any emails from Chatter.

Next, if you agree to receive emails (which is enabled by default), you can configure email settings and notifications for the **Personal** and **Group** setup.

We will not go through each option in the Personal setup, but they should be self-explanatory, such as if you want to be notified when someone follows you, someone post on your profile, likes your comment, mentions you, and so on. On this page, you also can set the frequency on how often you want to be notified, whether every single post or in the digest mode or never.

Email digests conveniently summarize recent activities in the Chatter, so you don't miss important discussions. You can choose to receive daily or weekly summaries of updates from your personal feed or any group's feed.

Daily digests include up to 50 of the latest posts from the previous day. **Weekly digests** include up to 50 of the latest posts from the week. All posts in each digest show their three latest comments. Chatter sends daily digests at approximately midnight every day, and weekly digests at approximately midnight on Sundays -- according to your personal time zone setting, to adjust your time zone in Salesforce, check out *Appendix, Setting Up My Salesforce* at the end of this book.

For the Personal setting, by default, all checkboxes are selected, and the frequency is **Daily digest**. For the Group setting, you can set your default frequency if you join or are added to a Group, by default, it is **Limited**, which means no email notifications, only receive emails for announcement posts in the group.

Note

Changing the default frequency for groups you join doesn't affect the groups you already belong to.

You can change the frequency of each Group that you joined, you should change the option to be more frequent for Groups that are more important for you to be stay updated or expect to contribute more.

Best Practices

- Do NOT turn off Chatter notification emails
- Enable receive email all types of notification
- Set the personal digest to Daily
- For Groups, set the frequency based on the importance of each group
  - » For super important groups, select Email in Each Post
  - » For important groups, select Daily Digests
  - » For not important groups, select Weekly Digests

Accessing Chatter

Chatter is part of the Salesforce platform; therefore, you need to login to Salesforce to be able to use it. You can collaborate using Chatter from multiple places:

- User Profile's detail page
- Record page
- Chatter tab
- Groups tab
- Mobile app
- Outlook/Gmail plugin
- Home page and Utility bar, only if your Salesforce admin add the Chatter component

All above are available by default unless your admin has removed them, except for the custom object, your Salesforce admin needs to manually add the component to the Lightning page. Each of them served a different purpose of collaboration and we will discuss each of the above items later in this chapter.

Chatter in User Profile's page

Every Salesforce user has their Profile page in Salesforce, which shows the summary of the user detail, the user's "About Me", and their avatar photo. To access and edit your Salesforce personal details, check out *Appendix, Setting Up My Salesforce* at the end of this book.

By default, every Salesforce user's Profile page includes **Chatter feed**, **Chatter Groups** (Groups of the user is a member of), **Following** (people that the user follows), and **Followers** (people that follow the user). As you see, this is very handy to access and is intuitive, as it is similar to many social media platforms.

When someone clicks your name on a record page, such as Account Owner, Opportunity Owner, etc., they will be landed on your Profile page, which containing your information and Chatter feed.

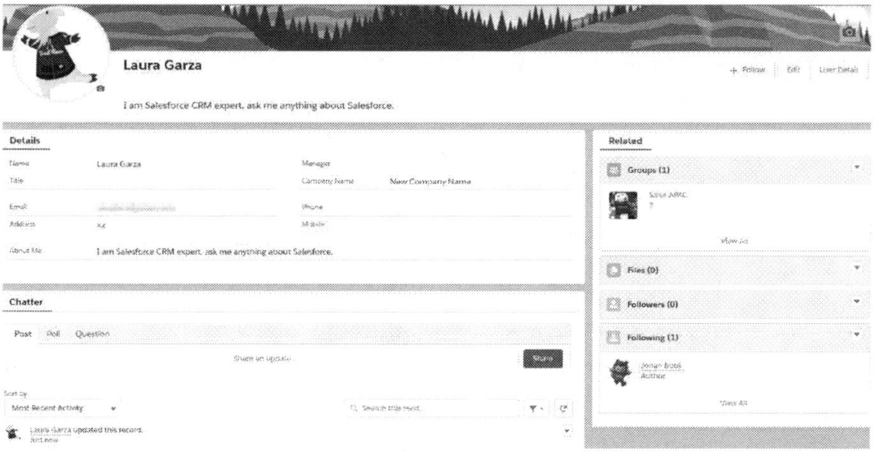

Figure 3.2 – User Detail with Chatter profile

> **Note**
>
> If you do not see Chatter feeds, Groups, Followers, and Following in your and other users' detail page, reach out to your Salesforce Admin. They may have removed it from the User's Profile page, or else Chatter may have been completely disabled in your Salesforce.

Following Users and Records with Chatter

In social media, you can follow artists that you like or important local/national news and institutions to get updates or announcements when they post. Similarly, in Salesforce, you can follow your colleagues to get their updates. So, every time they post or updates something in public visibility, you will be notified.

Additionally, you also can follow records, such as from Account, Opportunity, Contact, etc. By following the records that you are interested in, you will be notified when there are changes on those records, such as key customers owned by your team, or open opportunities with large amounts that are owned by your team members.

How to Follow Users

Following a user is pretty easy. You just need to open that user's profile page by searching the user name from Salesforce global search, or by clicking on the record owner, then click **+ Follow** button, then the button labels will change to **Following**.

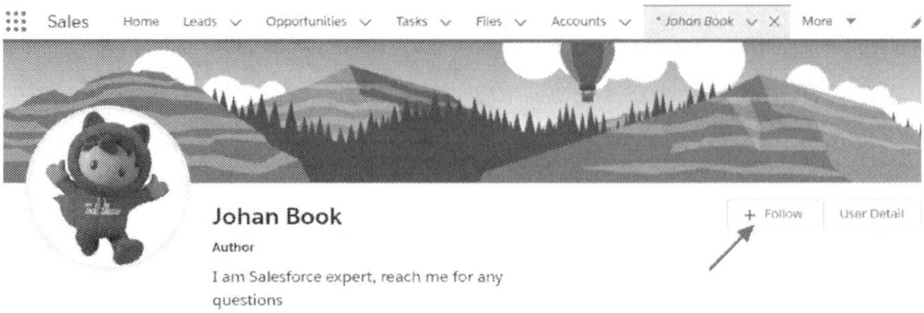

Figure 3.3 – Click + Follow button to follow the user

To **unfollow** a user, click the **Following** button and the label will change back to **+ Follow**. With this, you can easily confirm if you are following or not following a user.

How to Follow Records

Similar to following a user, following a record is pretty simple too, open the record that you want to follow, then click **+ Follow** button. Let's walk through how to follow a record, such as an opportunity:

1. Open the opportunity that you want to follow

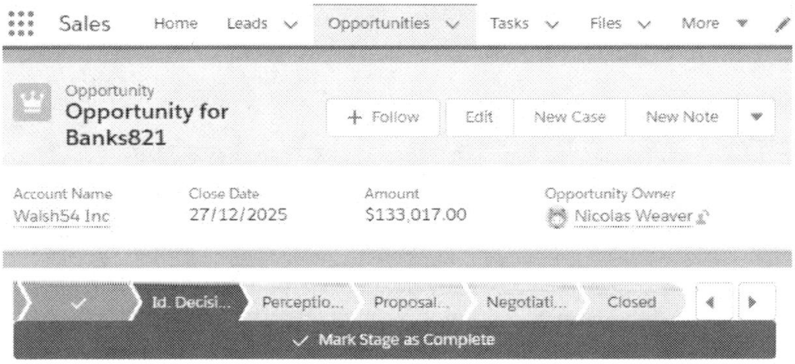

Figure 3.4 – Click + Follow button to follow the record

2. Click **+ Follow** button, and button with change to text **Following**

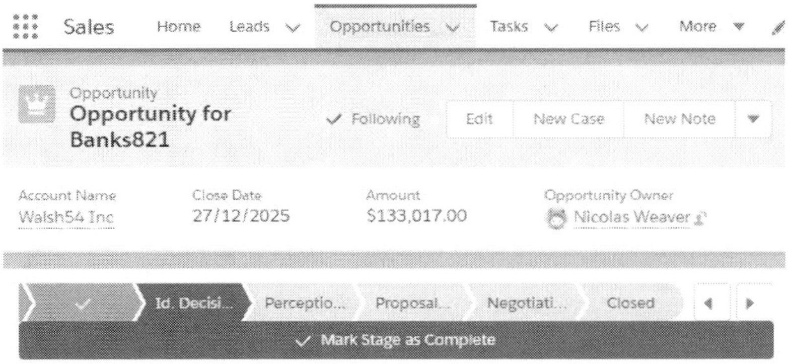

Figure 3.5 – Click Following to unfollow the record

The same as unfollow a user, to unfollow a record, click the **Following** button, and the label will change back to **+ Follow**. From here, you can easily see if you are following or not following that record.

> **Note**
>
> If you do not see the **Following** or **+ Follow** button on the record page, reach out to your Salesforce admin, your admin may have deactivated the object from **Feed Tracking** or hide the button from the Lightning page.

Auto Follow Records

Chatter also offers you the ability to automatically follow records that you created, to do so, use the following steps:

1. Click your avatar on the upper right corner of the Lightning page
2. Click **Settings** under your name
3. Under Chatter, click **My Feeds**
4. Select **Automatically follow records that I create**
5. Click **Save**

> **Note**
>
> There is a limit of 500 records and users that you can follow, if you need a higher limit, your Salesforce Admin can reach out to Salesforce to increase the limit to 2,000 records and users. If you need to mass unfollow users and records, your Salesforce Admin can mass unfollow records that you followed from the backend.

Chatter Group

Chatter Groups allow collaboration across all members within the group. But what does this type of collaboration mean? Similar to social media, in the Chatter Group, you can:

- Post, run a Poll, ask a Question, and make an Announcement
- Comment other users' posts and comments
- Like other users' posts or comments
- Share other users' posts or comments to other Groups or your followers
- Bookmark posts that you like
- Edit and delete your posts and comments

In terms of access type, there are 2 types of Chatter Groups:

1. **Public**, everyone can join the Group, see, and add posts, comments, and files.
2. **Private**, only group members can see and add posts, comments, and files. People must ask to join or be added by the group's owner or managers.

There is another type of Group called **Unlisted** Chatter Group, this Group offers more privacy than the Private Group as it doesn't even appear in search results.

If you're a group owner or manager, you can change groups from private to public, or from public to private by editing the group settings. If you change a private group to public, all posts and files will be visible to all users, all pending requests to join the group are accepted, and anyone can join the group.

There are 3 types of user membership in Chatter Groups:

1. **Manager**, this is similar to the administrator of the group. The manager can edit a group, add, or remove members, change the membership types of the members, and approve or reject the request to join the group
2. **Member**, standard group user
3. **Owner**, only one user can be the Group owner. By default, this is the user who creates the Group. The owner has similar permissions as the manager, but additionally, the owner can change the Group owner and delete the Group.

Chatter also offers the capability for users to post by sending emails, so each Chatter Group will have a unique email address. We will show you later in this chapter when we dive into the creation of a Chatter Group.

Accessing Chatter Groups

There are a few ways to access a Chatter Group:

1. Click the **Chatter** tab, then look for the Group name below **Recent Groups.** This will only show Groups you accessed recently.
2. Click the **Groups** tab. If you do not see the tab in the navigation bar, click the App Launcher (icon with the 9-dots at the further left of the navigation bar) and type Group. Check out *Chapter 1* on subchapter *Adding tabs to the Navigation Bar*, if you want to make Groups a permanent tab.
3. Type the Group name in the Global **Search** bar.
4. Access your Group by mobile app

Components of a Chatter Group

In the below screenshot, we show and explain all the components in a Chatter Group:

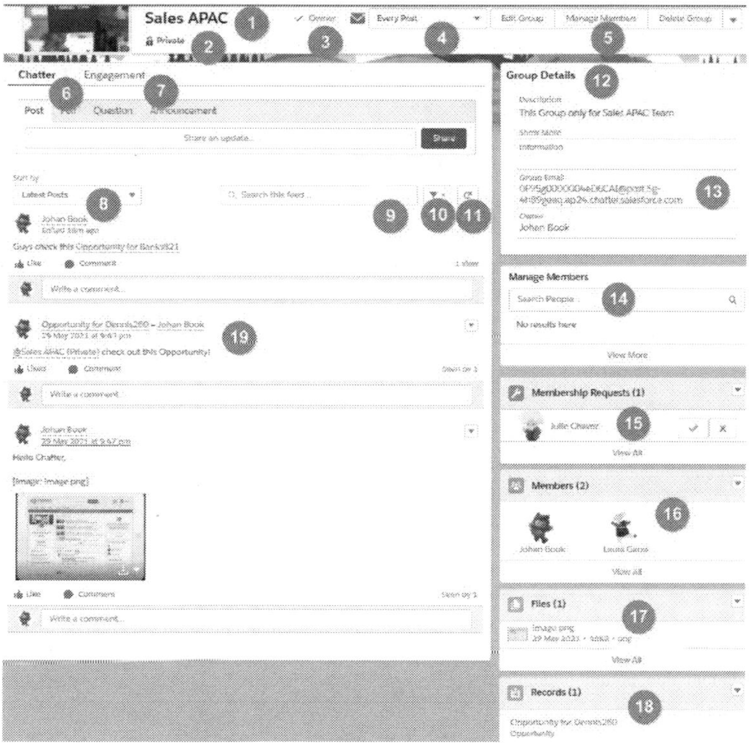

Figure 3.6 – Sample of a Chatter Group

1. Group Name
2. Information on the privacy of the group, whether it is Private or Public
3. User membership in that group
4. Where a user can manage their email notifications for that group
5. Buttons for Edit Group, Manager Members, Delete Group, only available for the Owner, while Edit Group and Manager Members buttons, available for the Group Manager
6. Chatter feed tab
7. Engagement tab, where you can see activities of the Group
8. Option to change feed sorting from Latest Posts (latest post to be added) to Most Recent Activity (latest post to be interacted with)
9. Search feed
10. Filtering feed – filter feeds from the default of All Updates, to filter to Unread Posts, All Questions, Unanswered Questions, Questions with No Best Answer, or Questions with Best Answer.
11. Refresh Chatter feed
12. Group Details information/description

13. Group Email, this is a unique email address to post from email
14. Manage Members panel, allows the Manager to add members
15. Membership Request will show users who request to access the Chatter Group
16. Members window will show all members in that Group, including their membership role
17. Files window will show all files uploaded to this Group
18. Records window show all records that mentioned this Group
19. Chatter feed panel

As in *Figure 3.6*, you can sort, search, filter, and refresh the Chatter feed.

Chatter Feed

All the posts in a Chatter Group will appear in the Chatter feed. You can make use of rich text format when posting, and the system also offers the capability to add images and attach files. Make use of emoticons when you post or comment to share your expressions 😊.

Like posts or comments to show your approval and receive email notifications if others comment on that post (unless you change this notification behavior in your personal settings). Below a post or comment, click **Like.** After you click **Like** on a post, the person who created the post is notified, and you receive email notifications if others comment on that post. If you click **Like** on a comment, the person who created the comment is notified, but you aren't notified about subsequent comments.

To stop liking a post or a comment, click **Liked** then the label will back to Like, after which you stop liking a post or a comment, you aren't notified about subsequent comments or likes. Likes on comments show how many people have liked the comment, e.g., "5 likes", to sees who is that 5 persons, click the "5 likes" link.

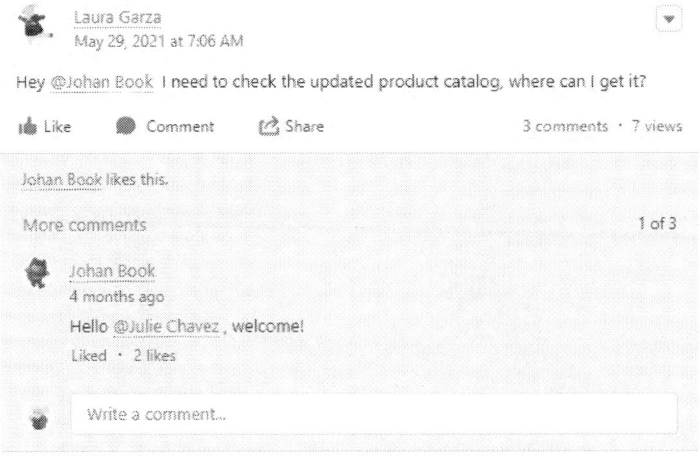

Figure 3.7 – Sample of Chatter feed

Bookmarking lets you keep track of individual posts you're interested in. After you have bookmarked a post, you can quickly find it from the **Bookmarked** tab. When someone comments on a post you bookmarked, you receive an email notification. Bookmarks are private, there is no limit on how many you can add, and other users can't see which posts you bookmark. When you are no longer interested in a post you saved, you can remove the bookmark.

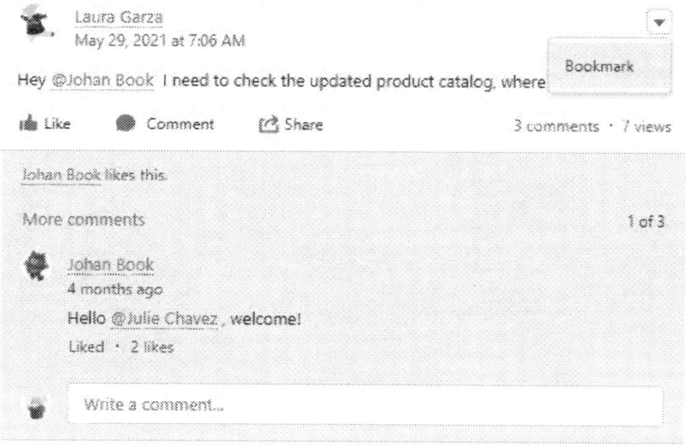

Figure 3.8 – Bookmarking a feed

To mention someone in order to draw their attention, enter **@** (the 'at' symbol) followed by the user's name, and to link the post to a record, enter **/** (the slash symbol) then type the record name. Depending on their notifications they will receive an alert in-app (Bell icon), by email, and on their Salesforce mobile app (if enabled by the owner).

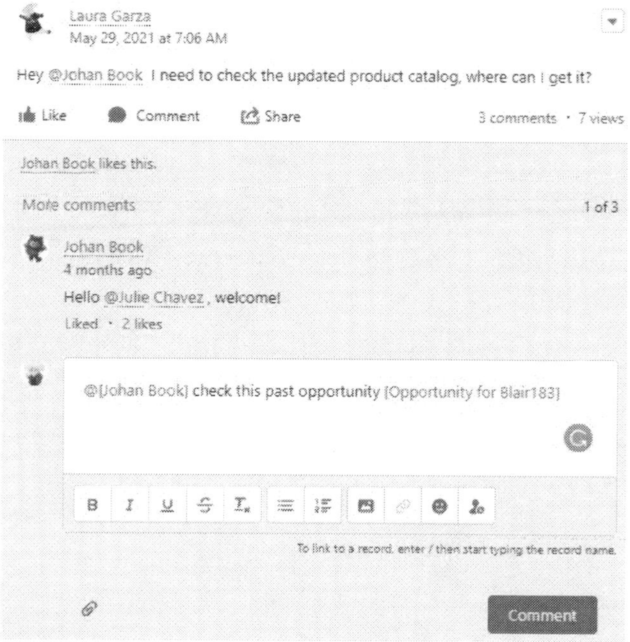

Figure 3.9 – Using @ and / in when Post or Comment

Posting a Poll

In Chatter feeds, you can also post **Polls** to conduct a survey, which is a great way to get people's opinions. It includes a list of choices in a feed post that lets people cast a vote by selecting one of the choices. Anybody with access to Chatter or the Poll can vote on the Poll, so always consider who you want to participate when you set the poll up, for example, inside a private Group, only the members of that Group can see the Poll and vote on the results. You can add up to 10 choices when setting it up but vote only once (although you can change your vote). Posts are anonymous, so you can see how many voted, but not who voted. Set the Poll up from the Poll tab in the Chatter feed.

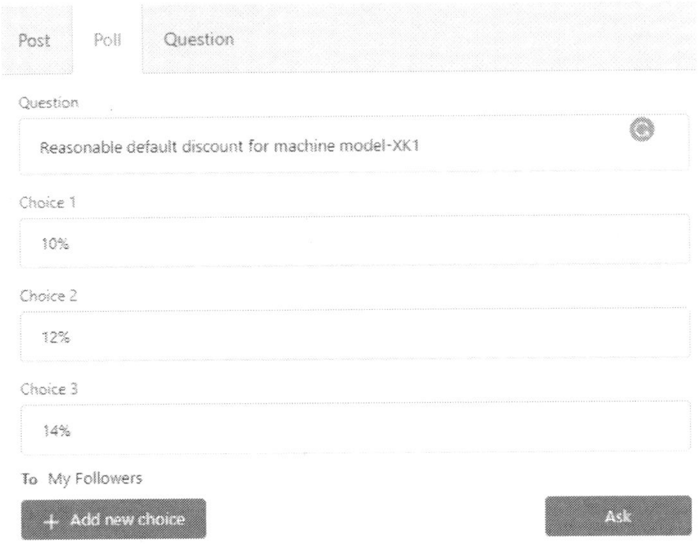

Figure 3.10 – Posting a Poll

Creating a New Chatter Group

You can create a new Chatter Group from the **Groups** tab or **Chatter** tab. Let's go through creating a new Chatter Group from the Groups tab.

1. Click the **Groups** tab, if you do not see it, click the App Launcher (9-dots icon) then type **Groups**
2. Click the **New** button at the upper right corner, if you do not see this button, reach out to your Salesforce Admin to grant you permission **Create and Own New Chatter Groups**.
3. Enter the following in the new Group window:
   - Name = "Global Product Support"
   - Description = "This group is the official support channel to reach the Product support team"
   - Information = "Global Product team Chatter Group"

- Access Type = Public
- Click **the Save & Next** button
- Upload an Image as the Group photo
- Click the **Next** button and **Done** button

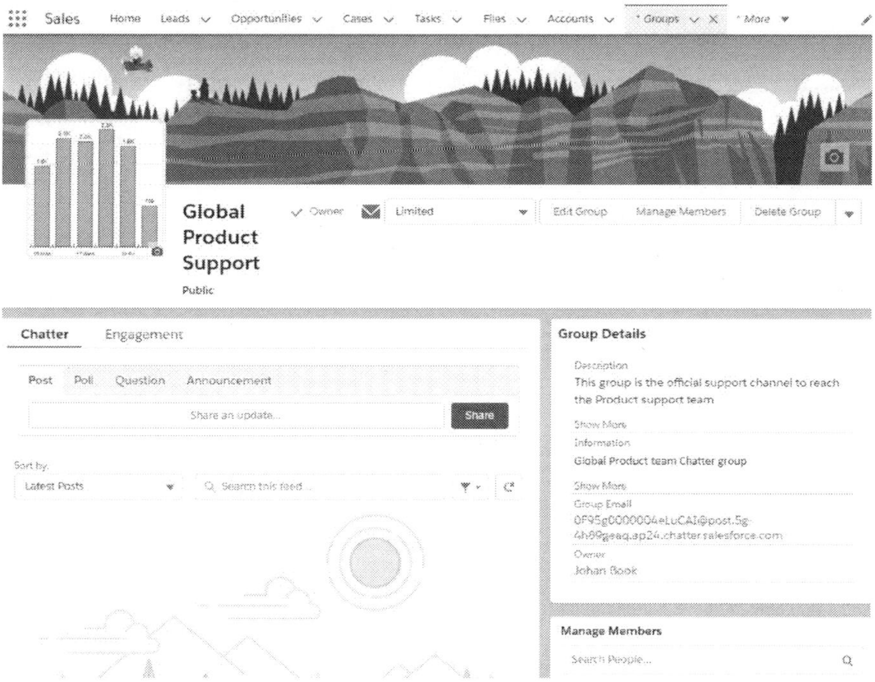

Figure 3.11 – A new Chatter Group

With just a few clicks, we have created a public Chatter Group that allows anyone in the organization to join and reach Global Product Support for questions, suggestions, etc.

> **Note**
>
> Chatter Group Name must be unique across public and private groups, including groups that have been archived. If a group is not enabled for automatic archiving, the group will be archived automatically, if the group has no new feed posts or comments for 90 consecutive days.

Chatter Tab

The Chatter tab combines all your Chatter feeds into one place, including:

- **What I Follow**, this will show all feeds for users and records that you followed
- **To Me**, this will show feeds where someone mentioned you in their post or comment

- **Bookmarked**, this will show feeds that you manually bookmarked
- **Company Highlights**, this will show you the most active posts in your organization
- **My Draft**, will show posts that have not yet been published. Posts will automatically save here if you click away from a post when midway through it, saving you time re-writing again.

When you click the Chatter tab, you will land on the **Company Highlights**. Sharing an update via Post, Poll, and Question from the Chatter tab will be visible for your **Followers**, while sharing updates in the Group will be visible to all members in the **Group**.

In the left panel of the Chatter tab, **Recent Groups** show the Group that you opened recently, so the list of Groups that appear here are different for each user. You can click the Group name to open it. You also can create a new Group by clicking the **+ icon** next to **Recent Groups.** The process to create a new Group is the same as creating one from the Groups tab as mentioned earlier.

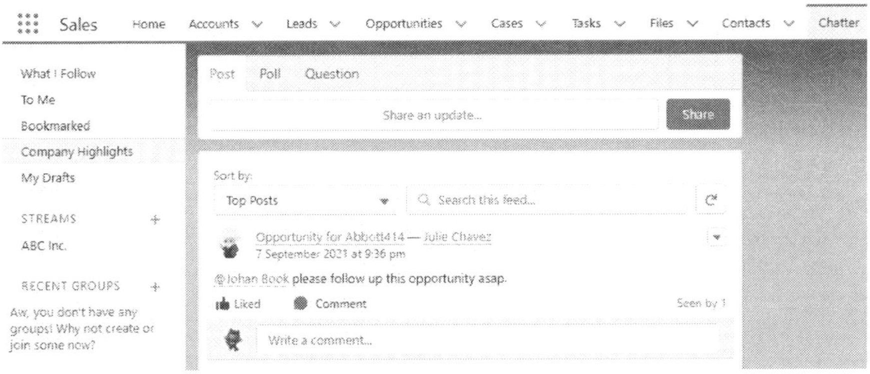

Figure 3.12 – Chatter tab

Chatter Streams

In the Chatter tab, above Recent Groups, there is a menu called **Streams**. How are these Streams related to Chatter? A stream will collect feeds from all records that are followed by that stream. It can be linked to records from different types of objects. This is very useful, for example, if you want to track multiple opportunities, accounts, contacts, etc., related to a parent company.

> **Note**
>
> Create up to 100 *streams* that combine posts from up to 25 different feeds and feed types.

How to access a Stream

Visit the Chatter feed workspace on the right-hand side to access your *streams* and click on the word **streams.** Here it lists all your streams and shows the people and records that you added. Each stream has its own row and its own set of row actions including **Edit** and **Delete**. Click the number of records on a row to see a full list of people and records that you added to the stream.

Click a stream name and open that stream. Once there, you can see the stream page has some actions. Use these to **edit** the stream, set up the **notifications,** and **delete** the stream. Each stream has a couple of filters under the funnel symbol. Choose **All Updates** to see everything, including Feed Tracked Changes (changes to objects and fields) in the stream. Choose **Fewer Updates** to omit these from the stream.

When you create a stream, **Every Post** option is available as the default for enabling notifications. Notifications are sent to you via email and pushed to your in-app notifications (if you have enabled this in your settings). Select **Never** to prevent notifications from this stream. You can adjust this from the stream page at any point.

Let us practice by creating a new Stream called `ABC Inc.` This Stream will contain all feeds from accounts and opportunities related to ABC Inc., even if the record name may not contain ABC. Let us start by clicking the **+ icon.**

1. Stream Name = `ABC Inc.`
2. Records to Follow, enter all accounts and opportunities that you would like to follow by this stream
3. Notify Me = Every Post
4. Click the **Save** button

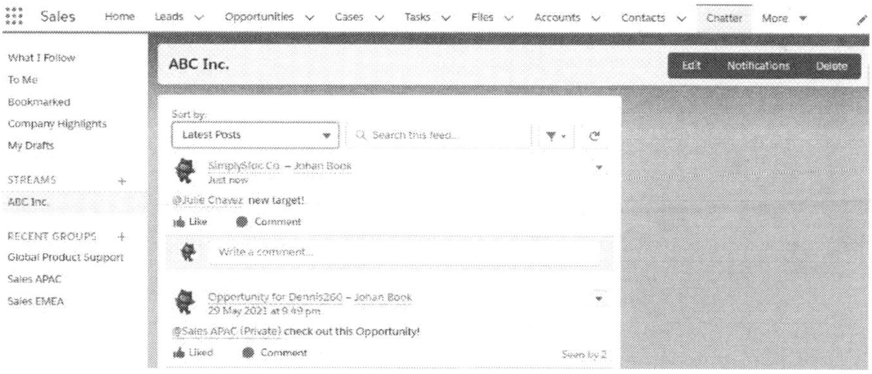

Figure 3.13 – A Chatter Stream

> **Note**
>
> If you need to add/remove records to follow in a stream, open the stream and click the Edit button, you can add/remove records to follow from here.

Records Feeds

As mentioned earlier in this chapter, we can follow a record to get updates and posts of that record. However, we also can see updates and collaboration on a record under the Chatter feed.

Every organization may design the Chatter component in a different area of the Lightning page, but by default, you should see **Post**, **Poll**, and **Questions** tab for this Chatter component. Similar to the post in Chatter Group, sharing updates in a record will allow users that have access to the record can see the post. Here is a sample of a post on the Account page:

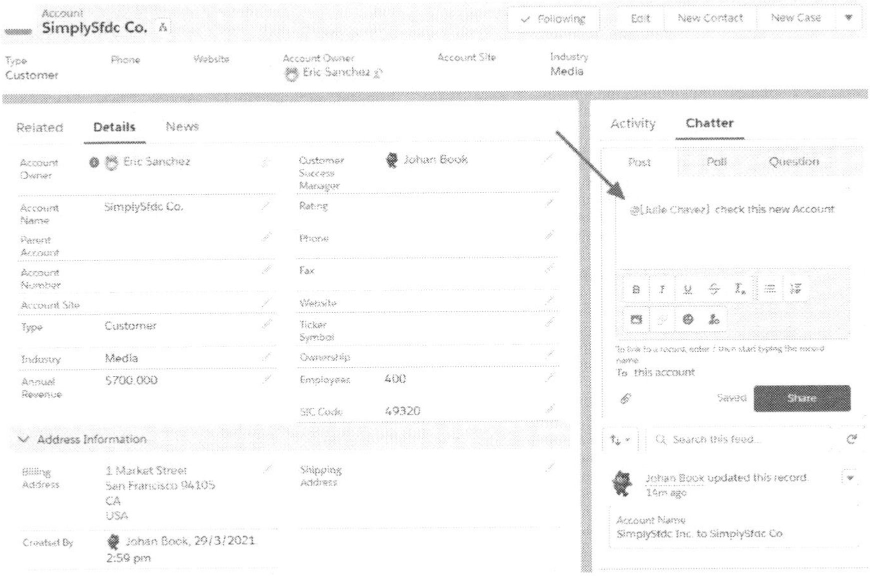

Figure 3.14 – Collaboration and update in the Account page

Summary

We have studied a lot about Chatter in this chapter, how we can collaborate in Salesforce, whether in a Group, a record page, or from the Chatter tab, so from now on, make use of Chatter to collaborate with your team members and colleagues.

Here are a few best practices when working in Chatter:

- Set your Chatter email notification as appropriate, this is to make sure you received important notifications on time, for Groups more critical to you, set the notification to Every Post.
- Follow social media collaboration ethics, such as not sharing personal matters in a public Group
- Follow coworkers and records that are important for you, so you don't miss anything you need to see

- Create a Chatter Group for your team member collaboration, or a Chatter Group to discuss a specific key customer.
- Make the Chatter tab visible in your navigation bar.

Bonus: Chatter Etiquette

DO

- Update your profile with a photo (preferably a professional headshot), as it creates a better connection between people who don't work face to face often. Check out *Appendix, Setting Up My Salesforce* if you are not sure how to update your Chatter photo.
- Keep your profile up to date if you change your title or when you are Out of Office.
- Participate by answering questions, liking, and commenting and help others
- @mention the person or @group to draw their attention to the right place, but don't overuse it
- Use a forward slash "/" to tag a correct record
- Use Chatter to point someone or group by posting inside the record, report, or dashboard
- Use hashtag "#" to relate important things together and enable quick search for topics
- Always post in short, sweet, and to the point
- Keep posts only for matters relevant to work
- Make use of text formatting and emoji to make your key points stand out in a longer post
- Add files, pictures, emojis, and links to your posts for a better engagement
- Use Chatter to ask for feedback, you can even create a poll and ask question
- Think before you post, realize your posts could be read by anyone in a record, profile, or public group
- Install the Salesforce mobile app, so you can collaborate from anywhere

DON'T

- Post
  - » anything that you wouldn't want to be seen by everyone in the company
  - » organization confidential information
  - » anything irrelevant to work or company
  - » something too personal and not suitable for company consumption

- Put down or belittle other people or use offensive language, even in the form of joke is not cool
- Use Chatter to replace in-person conversations
- Write a very long post – email is preferred for this

CHAPTER 4:

SEARCHING THE DATA

In this chapter, we will discuss **Search** in the Salesforce platform and how to get the most out of this function. We search for a word in Microsoft Word or Google Docs, search for a file name in Windows or macOS, and search in Salesforce is just as useful and powerful. One of the best features in Salesforce is the search capability, it offers an intelligent and simple way to find data in Salesforce fast and efficiently.

We will go through these main topics in this chapter:

- How to search
- Refine Search Results
- View More and Show More
- How to modify search results
- Searchable Data
- Einstein Search

How to Search

It is pretty simple to search in the Salesforce Lightning platform. Salesforce provides a textbox at the top center of the page, called **Global Search**. Similar to the Favorites functionality, the global search is available anywhere within the Salesforce Lightning platform.

If you click your mouse in the global search box, the system will show five items that you opened recently, allowing you to quickly re-open items that were recently opened by you.

To start searching, simply type in the text you want to search in the search box, it can be Account Name, Contact Name, Opportunity Name, or any other key fields, and you will get the result instantly. Even as you type, Salesforce will attempt to work out potential matches for your search in the dropdown, particularly any records that you recently accessed.

Once you finish typing, the system will give you a list of top results from **All** objects that you used often, but if you want to search only from a specific object, such as Accounts, you can filter to search from that object only, simply click the **All arrow** before the global search box, to select the object.

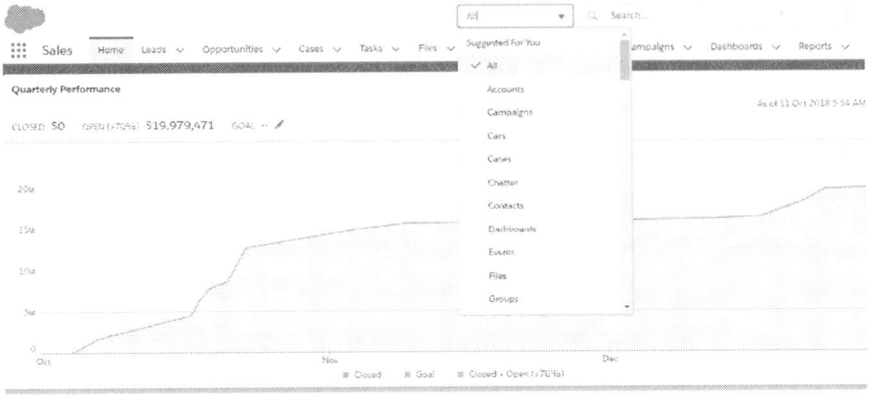

Figure 4.1 – Global search box

For example, as per *Figure 4.1*, to get the result from Account, simply select **Accounts**, instead of the default **All**. The benefit being, you will get results faster and you can refine the result directly in the search result window.

If you do not see the record that you are looking for, simply hit the Enter key, or click the magnifying glass icon or text in the search box.

> **Tips**
>
> Searching in Salesforce is not **case-sensitive**, for example, searching Acme and acme will give you the same result.

Refine Search Results

We just discussed how to search in Salesforce, however, if the result returned is large, like 100 or more records, we need some time to find the correct data that we are looking for. Instead of manually using your eye to go through each of them, Salesforce allows you to refine the results based on the fields that will appear. Here is a quick hands-on example to search for an Account:

1. Enter an Account Name to search. In my example, I'll type Acme, but you can search any account that you have.
2. Since I know that I am only searching in the Account object, select **Account** before the search box.

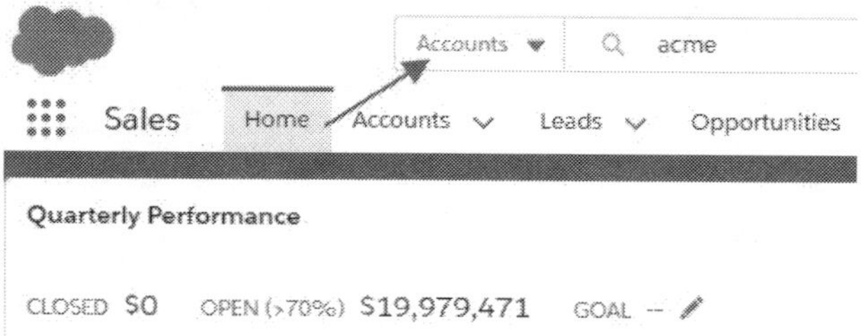

Figure 4.2 – Select Account and type acme

3. Another option to search only in the Account object is by clicking the Accounts tab, type `acme`, then select **"acme" in Accounts**, this will produce the same result as (2).

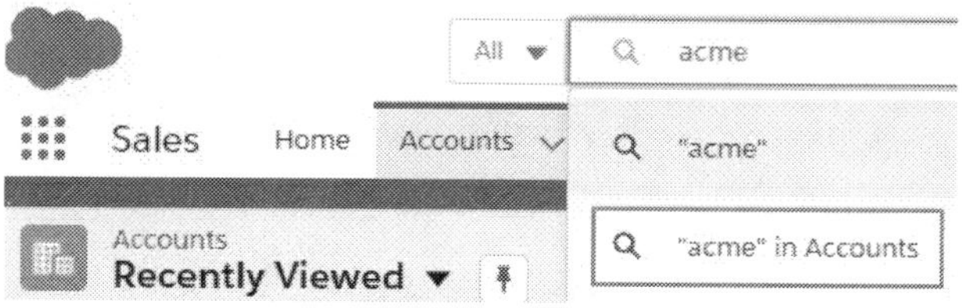

Figure 4.3 – Search from the Account tab

4. Search will return up to 50 records and sort by Relevance, you can change the sorting by clicking **Relevance** or click the column header to sort by that field. If you have more than 50 records in the search result, you can keep scrolling down and Salesforce will expose another 50 records.

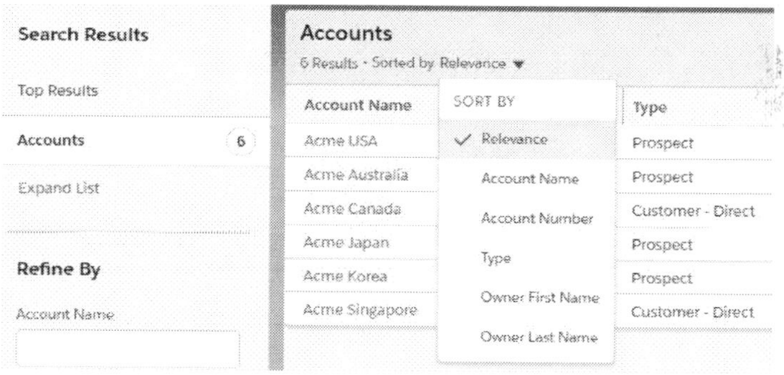

Figure 4.4 – Change sort result

5. To refine the search result; look at the left panel where you will see **Refine By**, then you will find a list of fields that are the same as search result columns. From here, you can filter further to filter results only based on the selection in that panel, the search result will be updated immediately.

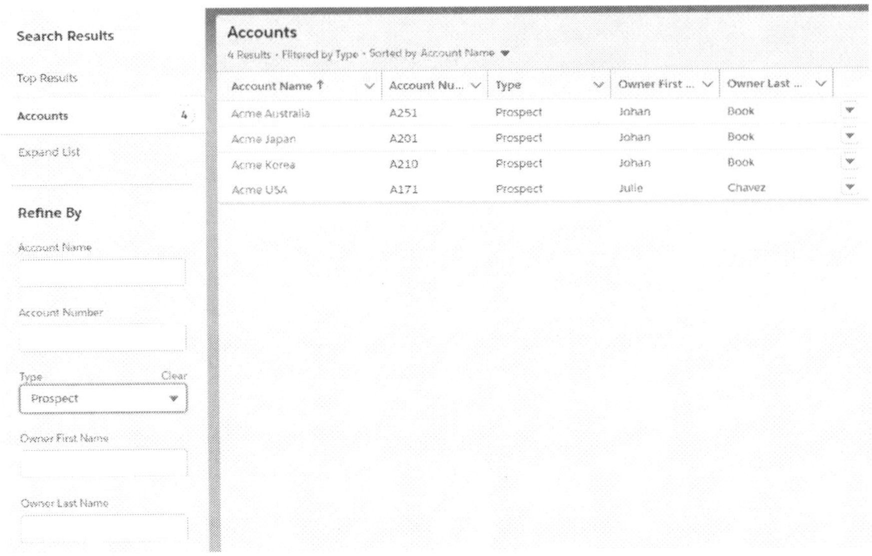

Figure 4.5 – Change sort result

6. Next, you can simply open, or edit the record by clicking the arrow button at the further right of the record.

By refining the search results, you can search faster, and increase your productivity. To search all results, click **Expand List** link on the left panel under the Object name, in our example here, the Object is Accounts.

View More and Show More

If you do not know which object has the records that you are looking for, just type in the global search box and hit enter, which will take a bit more time, because Salesforce will search all objects that you use frequently. The search result will show only five records for each object, so if you do not see the record you are looking for in an object, simply click the **View More** link on the upper right section in the Object result.

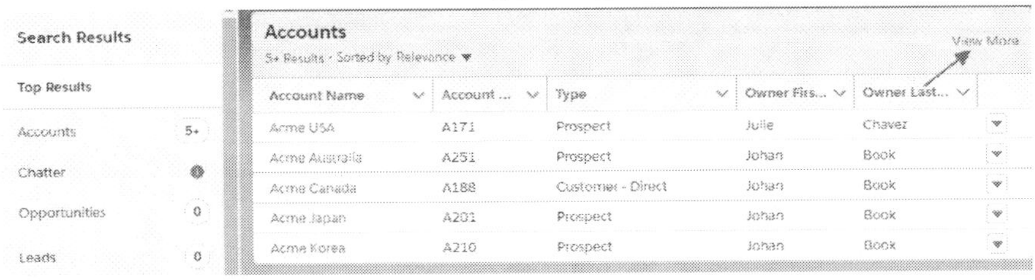

Figure 4.6 – Click View More to view more records from that object

After clicking View More, the result will be filtered just from an object. This is similar to searching for an object discussed in our previous hands-on exercise, and then you can refine the result as necessary.

Notice that I mentioned when we hit search to all objects, Salesforce will search all objects that you use **frequently**. This means, even if you search All, the system will only search objects based on your usage in Salesforce, as the system remembers objects that you use frequently. For example, if you only access Account, Contact, and Opportunity in your daily job, Salesforce will not search other Objects such as Work Orders. This is useful because the system will get the result faster by only searching amongst those objects.

However, in case you need to see the result from all objects, at the lower-left corner of the search result, click the **Show More** link, now the system will search all objects that you have accessed.

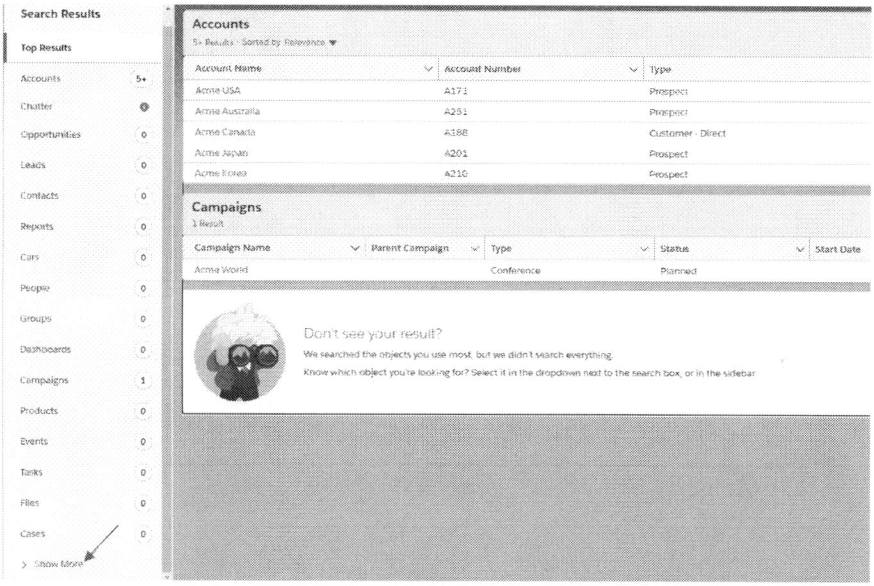

Figure 4.7 – Click Show More to search all objects

You need to click the object name to see the result, for my example, I click the **Work Orders** tab to see results from that object.

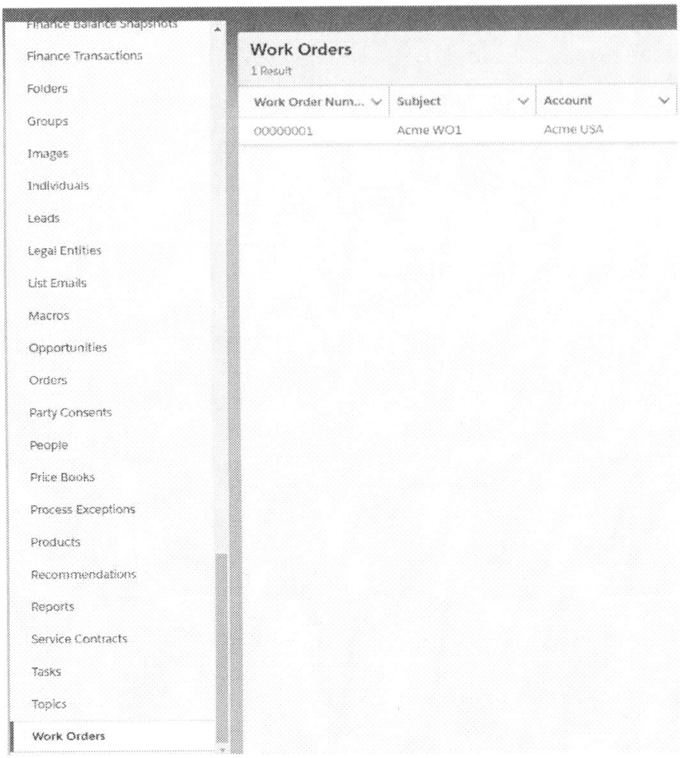

Figure 4.8 – Click the object name to see the result

So, when you do not see your search result, don't panic:

1. Click **View More**, to see all records from the object
2. Click **Show More**, to let the system search all objects, then click the object name.

If you still can't find the record after click View More and Show More, there may be a few reasons:

1. The record is newly entered, so it's still being added to the index. When you create or update a record, all the searchable content gets added to the index, which usually takes a few minutes but can take up to 15 minutes.
2. Not all objects and fields are searchable and you're trying to find a record with a field that isn't searchable, such as a formula field is not searchable.
3. The text is spelled or entered wrongly or slightly differently, maybe it is the same but without spaces. Although search is intelligent, it does not always bring up varieties of names.
4. You don't have access to the record. Global search only returns results you have permission to view. If you do not have permission to view the folder a report is stored in, for example, you will not be able to see it.

5. Ensure the object has a tab created. Objects without a tab aren't returned in search results, and the Tab visibility must be set to 'Default On' or 'Default Off'. If doubt, check this with your Salesforce admin.

Modify Search Results

The data you see in the search results will only be data that you have permission to access. You will not gain extra visibility from the search results; it is the same as direct access to the record or from a report. So, given above, can we modify what we see in the search results in Salesforce? Yes and No, depending on how you interpret it:

No – as stated above, you will not gain any extra access from the search results

Yes – you can refine the search results (as discussed in the earlier subchapter) and you can request your Salesforce admin to update the columns available in the search results.

Refer to *Figure 4.5* as a sample, we have five fields in the search result: Account Name, Account Number, Type, Owner First Name, and Owner Last Name. Your Salesforce Admin can add or remove the fields that show in the search results, which are the same fields for refining the search.

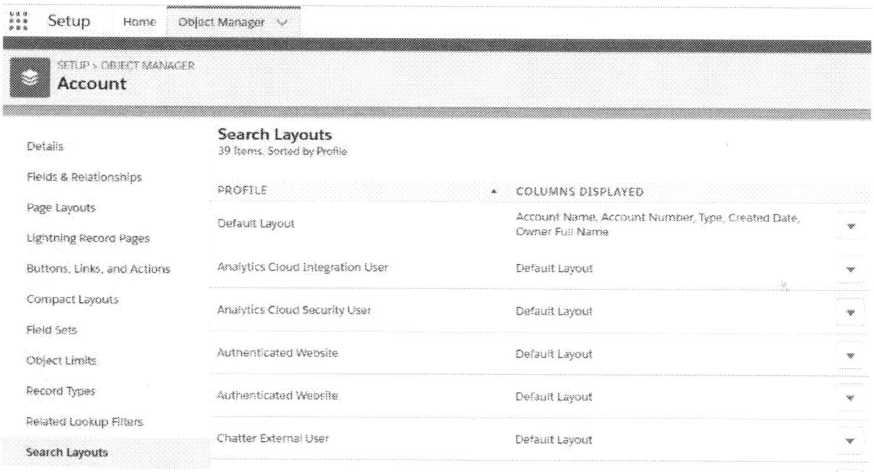

Figure 4.9 – Salesforce Admin able to change columns displayed in search by Profiles

> **Notes**
>
> For Salesforce admins, changing fields in the **Default Layout** profile for the **Search Layout** will change the fields that show in the **Recently Viewed** list too. If the different teams need to see different columns in the search result, update the fields by user profile in the Search Layout.

As per *Figure 4.9*, for example, if your Salesforce admin removes Owner First Name and Owner Last Name, then adds Created Date and Owner Full Name.

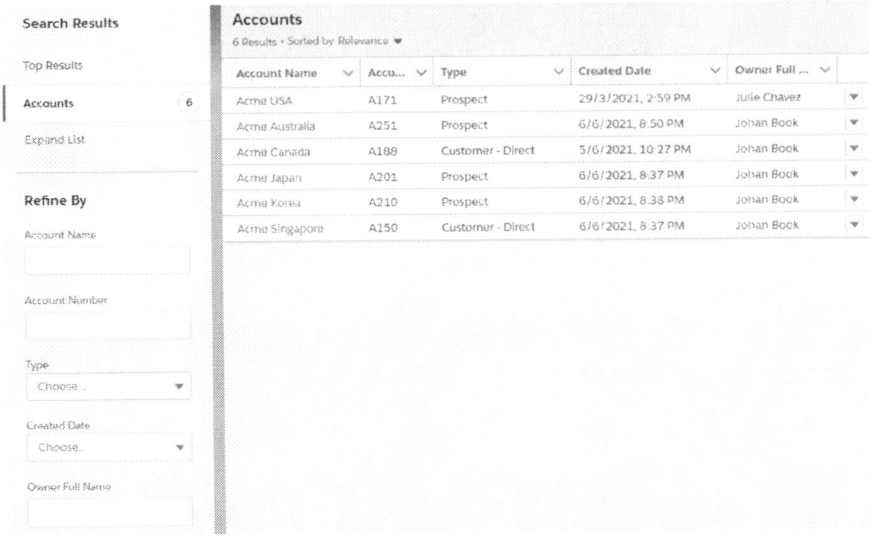

Figure 4.10 – Updated columns of search result and Refine By

Because of the changes performed by your Salesforce admin on the **Default Layout**, refer to *Figure 4.9* again, this change will also update the columns in the **Recently Viewed** list view for that Object.

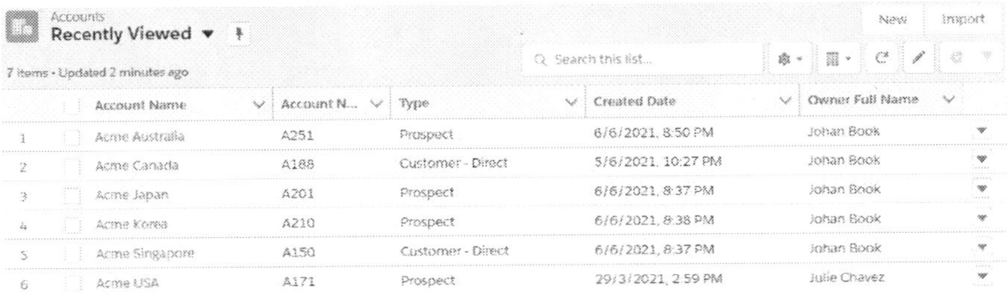

Figure 4.11 – Columns updated too in Recently Viewed list view

Searchable Data Type

To make an object searchable, there are a few items that your Salesforce admin need to perform:

- All standard objects such as Account, Contact, Opportunity, Lead, Campaign, and Case are searchable by default. For custom objects, the **Allow Search** option must be enabled for the object.
- Ensure the object has a tab created
- Tab visibility for the user's assigned Profile is not Tab Hidden

If the object is enabled and configured correctly for search for objects that you have access to, you should be able to search the fields, even if the field is not added to your page layout. This can happen if the data is populated by the backend integration or populated by other users using different page layouts.

Note

Formula fields are not searchable, simply because they are not stored in the database, they will be calculated on the fly when accessed. The formula field is calculated based on other fields defined, and the value is not editable by the user. If you are unsure, check out with your Salesforce admin if a particular field is a formula field.

For **standard objects**, not all fields are searchable, please refer to this article for all searchable fields *https://help.salesforce.com/articleView?id=sf.search_fields_lex.htm&type=5*. As you can see from that article, all Name fields are searchable. For **custom fields** in the standard objects, only the following type of fields are searchable:

- Auto Number
- Email
- Phone
- Text, Text Area, Text Area (Long), and Text Area (Rich)

For **custom objects**, the searchable fields are the same as custom fields in the standard object, which are auto number, email, phone, text, text area, text area (long), and text area (rich).

Best Practice

Always enter the meaningful or right name for a record, as that will impact your search results, such as for Opportunity Name, Case Subject, Account Description, and so on. The best is to have a standard naming convention and governance across all users in the company.

Einstein Search

Salesforce search has recently become even more powerful and intelligent with Einstein Search. It is a new feature offered by Salesforce to boost user productivity when searching and is built using Artificial Intelligence technology. The good news is that it is available for all customers without additional licenses or costs. If your organization does not yet have the use of Einstein Search in Salesforce, reach out to your Salesforce admin to enable it.

So, what is the difference between Einstein Search and the default search discussed earlier in this chapter, and how can Einstein Search help boost your productivity?

Firstly, Einstein Search will not let you search data that you don't have visibility of, so the basic principle is maintained. There are three features offered by Einstein Search and we will discuss all of them in detail in this subchapter:

1. Personalization
2. Natural Language Search
3. Actionable Instant Results

Personalization

The search result is personalized based on your activity, location, ownership, and industry as a user. Without Einstein Search, all users will see the same result when searching with the same keyword. While with Einstein Search, the search result order is personalized and based on relevance to each user.

Einstein Search learns how you use the system daily and offers search results based on your data and activity. For example, if you are based in Singapore and search for `Acme` accounts, your search result will likely show Acme accounts with addresses in Singapore as the top result.

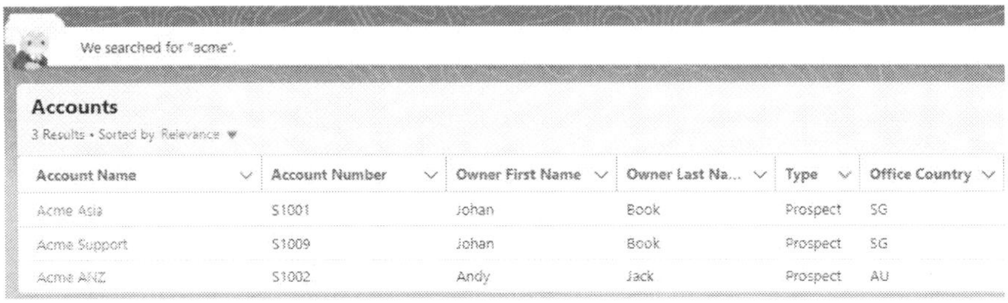

Figure 4.12 – Einstein search results personalized to each user

> **Notes**
>
> Personalization of search results applied for accounts, contacts, opportunities, cases, and leads.

Natural Language Search

With the use of Natural Language Search functionality, you just need to type the common phrases in the global search box, such as `my open opportunities`, `Johan accounts`, `cases closed last week`, to receive the results you are after. Natural language search is case insensitive.

In this scenario, my boss would like to check all Accounts owned by me without running a report, with Einstein Search my boss just needs to type `johan book accounts and they will be exposed in search results`

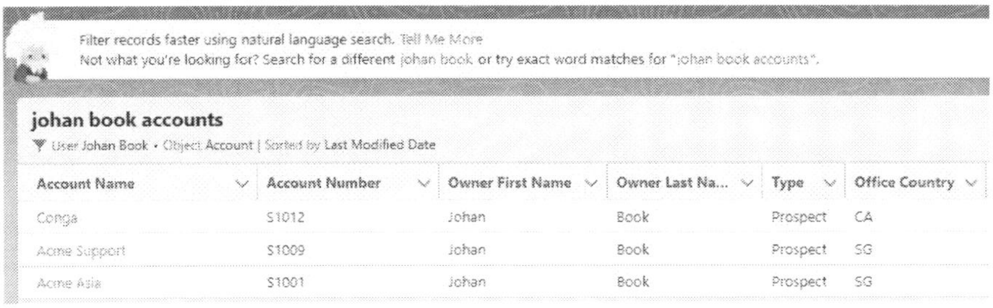

Figure 4.13 – Natural Language Search result

Check out this document for more examples of natural language search: *https://help.salesforce.com/articleView?id=sf.search_ai_natural_lang_examples.htm&type=5*

Same as personalization, Natural Language Search can be used for accounts, contacts, opportunities, cases, and leads too.

Actionable Instant Results

As previously mentioned, in standard search, clicking the search box will show you the last five records accessed, then you click the record to open it. Einstein Search allows you to do more, you can drill down to the record details and related information of the record without type or click anything, simply hover your mouse over the record to see actionable instant results.

For example, I simply hover my mouse on `Acme Asia`:

- I can see the summary for `Acme Asia`
- I can follow, and edit the `Acme Asia` account, without opening the `Acme Asia` record
- I also see all related lists for the `Acme Asia` account. I can see how many contacts, opportunities, etc. that are linked to the `Acme Asia` account.

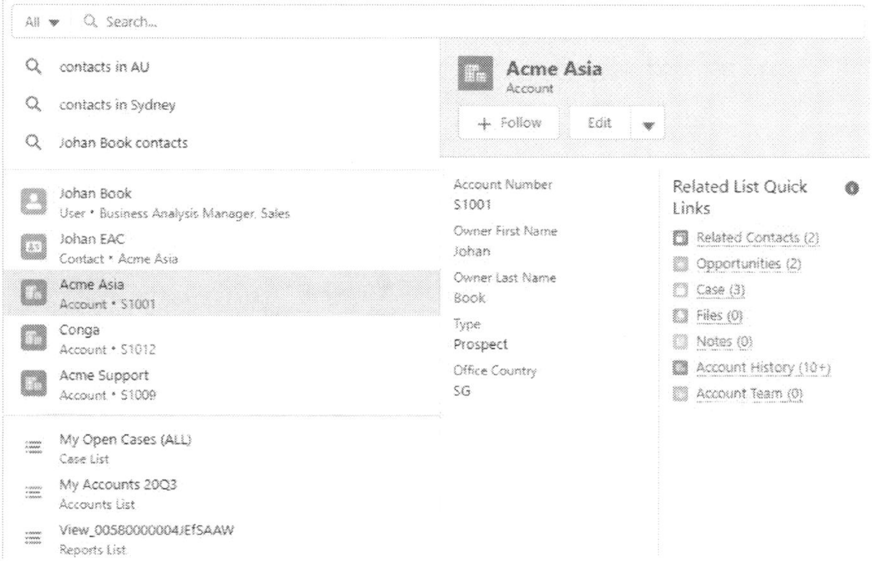

Figure 4.14 – Actionable Instant results with Einstein Search

- Next, I hover my mouse over Opportunities in the related list quick links and I'll be able to see the Opportunities summary, right from the search box.

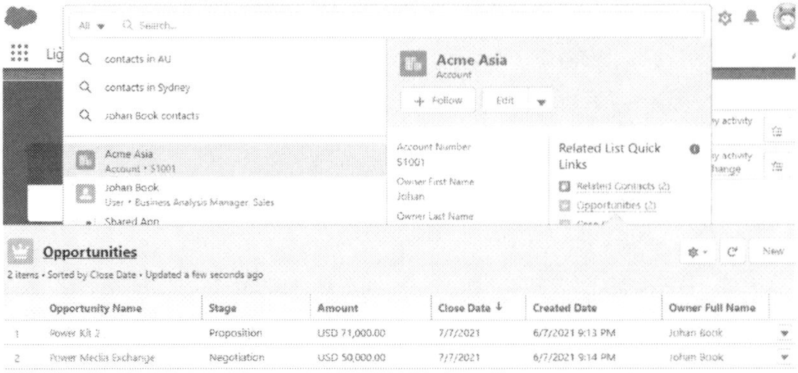

Figure 4.15 – View Opportunities from Account

All the above actions are performed **without a single click**, just by hovering the mouse over Acme Asia in the search box.

When you type in the search box, Einstein will also show the results of the top five records instantly, based on the keyword entered and how you personally use Salesforce. Same here, you can hover the mouse over each record to get actionable instant results. If you need to search further, just hit the **Enter** key for the system to show results that personalize for you.

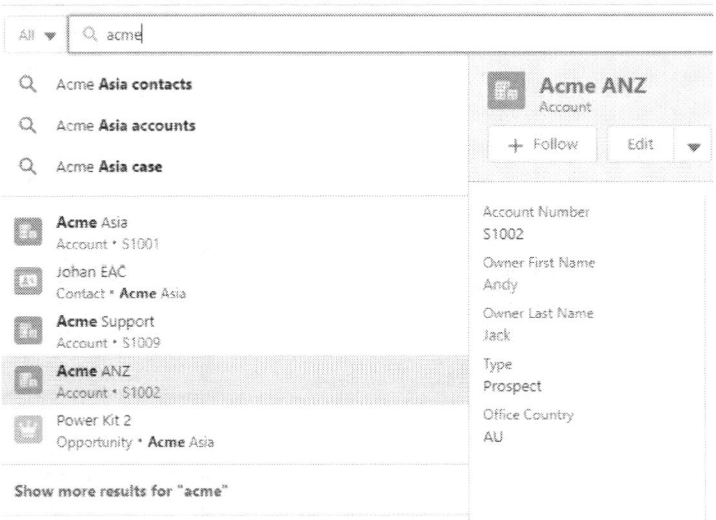

Figure 4.16 – Same actionable instant result when entering a specific keyword

Einstein search can also return similar results by applying features such as spell correction, allowing nicknames and special characters, synonym groups (if enabled by Salesforce admin), and matching other forms of a word or when the names contain part of the entered term.

Wildcards and Operators for Search

Some helpful wildcards and operators to help you filter when searching:

- Asterix (*) - find items that match zero or more characters in the middle or at the end of your query, e.g. Acme* will search all Name start with Acme, such as Acme Canada, Acme USA, etc.
- Question mark (?) - to match only one character in the middle or at end of your query. e.g., Acme Kore? will return the result of Acme Korea, but Acme K? will not return any result.
- AND - to match ALL search terms included. e.g., acme and world will return records with keywords contain both acme and world, the keyword can be in any searchable field.
- OR - to match at least one of the search terms, e.g., acme or world will return records that contain acme or world, the keyword can be in any searchable field.
- AND NOT - to match the first keyword, but doesn't contain the second keyword, e.g., acme and not japan will return all acme records that do not have japan in any searchable fields.
- Parentheses ()- to group terms with logical operators e.g. (acme and not japan) or off will return all acme records that do not have japan in any searchable fields, and records that contain off in the searchable fields
- Quotation marks (") - to search items to find matches in the order you enter the terms. e.g., "acme japan" will return all acme japan records, such as Acme Japan, Acme Japan Inc, but will not return records such as Acme Inc Japan.

Summary

In this chapter, we learned how to perform a search, how to refine search results, how to use View More and Show More links, how to modify columns in the search result. We also learned what type of data is searchable, we end this chapter with a new cool search feature powered by Artificial Intelligence called Einstein Search, then we also learned about using wildcards and operations in search keywords to get a better search result.

Here are the best practices when performing a search:

- If you know which Object you are searching for, filter just to search on that Object, it is faster and allows you to refine the results faster.
- Salesforce remembers the Objects and records that you access the most, so if you do not see the result you want, use the View More and Show More links.
- Consult with your Salesforce admin to show only the most important fields in the search results.
- Not all data is searchable, but as we learned, the Name field is searchable in all objects, so make sure to enter the name that reflects the record correctly, such as Opportunity Name. Consider working with your colleagues to develop

naming conventions with unique names where possible to make it easier to find what you need faster.

- Make use of Einstein Search to boost your search results, reduce clicks and get actionable instantly right from the search box.
- Make use of wildcards and operations in search keywords to get a better search result.

By now, you should be able to search more efficiently, know how best to make the most of the search methodology, and understand the searchable fields.

CHAPTER 5:

REPORTING ON THE CLOUD

Reporting is one of the most powerful and used features across all Salesforce users, whether you are a sales rep, a sales support user, a sales manager, or another business user. So, make sure you make use of the reporting functionality, with the help of advice from this and the next chapter.

The best of Salesforce reporting is the ease of building and maintaining reports, and the collaboration available with sharing reports with other team members and managers. When you run a report, you will receive instant results and insights into data currently stored in your Salesforce instance.

Here are the main topics that we will go through in this chapter:

- Sharing with Report Folders
- Building with Report Types
- Creating a Report from scratch
- Joined Reports
- Inline Editing in a Report

Sharing with Report Folders

Before we start creating a report, we need to learn about the structure of Salesforce reporting. We need to ask ourselves, if we need to store a report after it has been created? Well, your answer may depend:

- No, if the report is for one-off or ad-hoc purposes e.g., if you do not need the run it again in the future
- Yes, if you plan to run the report again in the future, or if you plan to share the report with your team

If you do plan to save the report, where will the report be stored? There are three possible categories when you store a report:

1. Private Reports folder
2. Public Reports folder
3. Shared folders

Before we discuss further the difference between each of those folder types, please note that the report folder category choice also determines who can access those reports.

> **Notes**
>
> Report accessibility is not determined on the report itself, but on where the report is stored.

Private Reports folder

Treat the Private Reports folder as your own personal folder, as no one else can edit or delete reports stored in this folder (not even your Salesforce admin), but on top of this, no one else can access or run reports stored here, so you cannot share a report with your team if it is stored in your Private folder.

When you save a new report, the default option is to store it in the **Private Reports** folder.

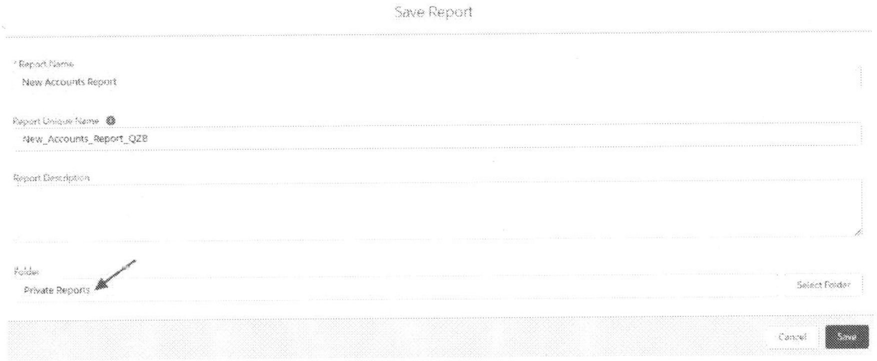

Figure 5.1 – Selecting report folder when saving a report

You can access reports in the **Private Reports** folder from the **Reports** tab in the navigation menu. Click the **Reports** tab, then look for **Private Reports** at the left panel.

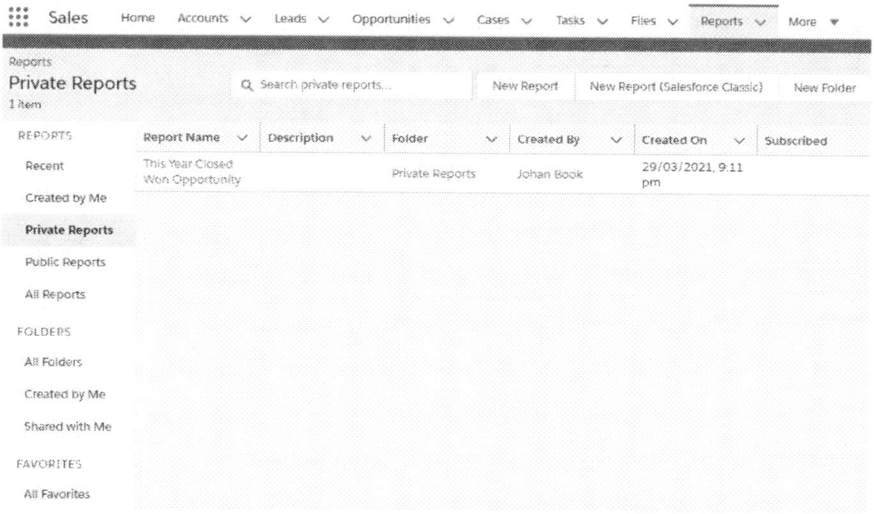

Figure 5.2 – Private Reports will show all reports stored in your Private Reports folder

> **Tips**
>
> Use this private folder if you are running reports for your own personal use only. Remember to keep this folder maintained by deleting any reports you ran that you no longer need again.

Public Reports folder

The Public Report folder is the opposite of the Private Report folder, in that everyone can store their reports in this folder. It also gives everyone access to run reports stored in this folder, no matter who has created the report. Although all users can run the reports stored here, it doesn't mean all users will get the same result when they run the report. The result is based on the users' permission to see the data stored in Salesforce.

Also, this does not mean all users can edit and delete reports stored here. They will be able to use Save As to clone the report as a new report, but not overwrite it. Only the report creator, Salesforce admin, and users with **Manage Reports in Public Folders** permission will be able to edit and delete reports stored here.

How about if I want to share a report with my team, should I store the report here?

Well, it depends:

- Yes, if the report is not confidential, only being used for a short period, and needs to be accessed by cross-functional users on an ad-hoc basis.
- No, if it is exposing confidential data, or will need to be used in the future. Then, the report should be stored in a shared folder.

You can find all reports stored in the **Public Reports** folder exactly below the **Private Reports** tab, you can refer to *Figure 5.2*.

Sharing with Report Folders

The purpose of Shared Folders is to give accessibility to a select group of users. You need to have **Create Report Folders** permission for the ability to create report folders, otherwise, you will not see the **New Folder** button.

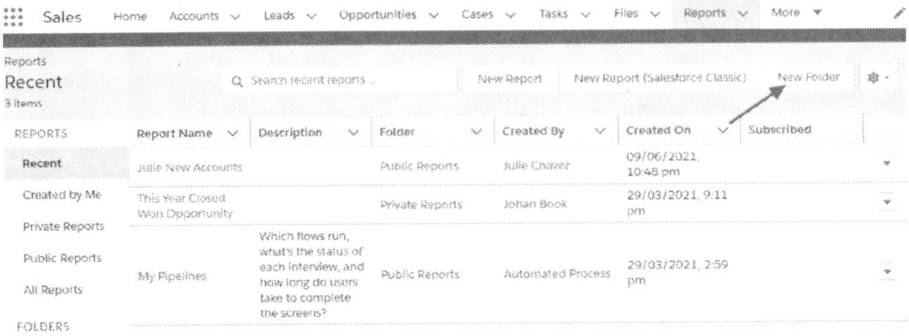

Figure 5.3 – New Folder button under Reports tab

Let's get hands-on to create a report folder, for example, EMEA Sales and share it with your team members:

1. Click the **Reports** tab in the navigation menu
2. Click the **New Folder** button
3. Type `EMEA Sales` in the Folder Label, then click on textbox Folder Unique Name, the value in this textbox will be auto populated
4. Click the **Save** button

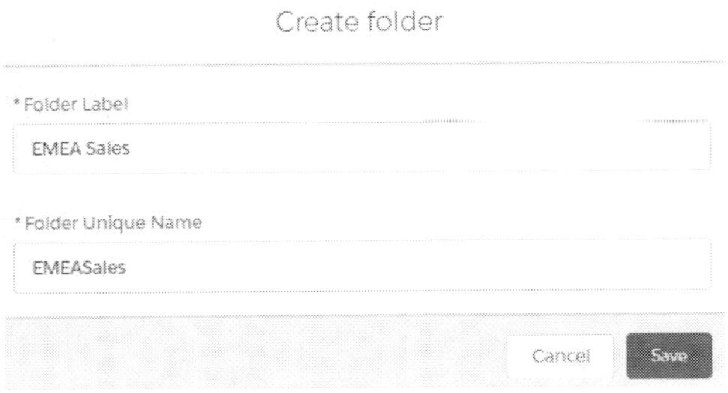

Figure 5.4 – Creating a new Report Folder

5. Now the report folder has been created, let's share it with your team. Click the arrow icon before the gear icon, then select **Share**

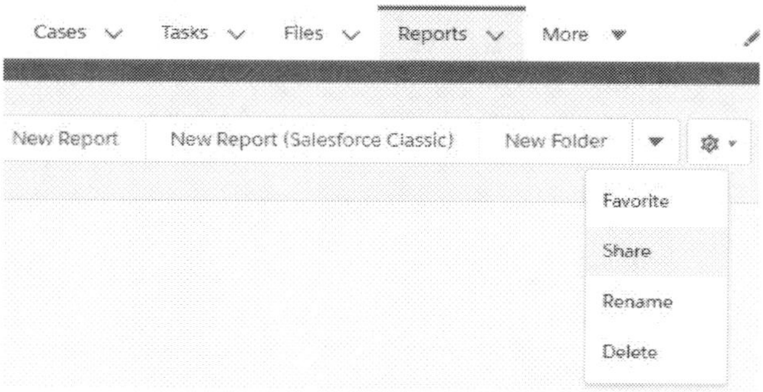

Figure 5.5 – Menu to share Report Folder

> **Tips**
>
> You also can open the Share folders window from the Report tab, select **All Folders** or **Created By Me** or **Shared with me**, looks for the folder that you want to share, or type in the **Search all folders** box. On the report folder list, select the arrow at the further right of the folder and click **Share**.

6. You now have the option to share the report folder to:
   - Users
   - Roles
   - Roles and Subordinates
   - Public Groups
   - If your Salesforce is enabled with Enterprise Territory Management, you can share the folder to Territories, and "Territories and Subordinates" too.
7. Next to the Name is the **Access** setting (*check Figure 5.6*), here the user, role, or group can access the folder with the following permission:
   - **View**: able to view or run reports stored in the folder
   - **Edit**: In addition to View, users are able to edit existing reports stored in this folder and create new reports to store in this folder
   - **Manage**: In addition to Edit, users with Manage access are also able to manage sharing access, rename the folder name and delete the folder.
8. For this exercise, as you see in *Figure 5.6* below, I'll give a user edit access, and add the ability for the CEO roles to view the reports in that folder.
9. Click the **Done** button to close

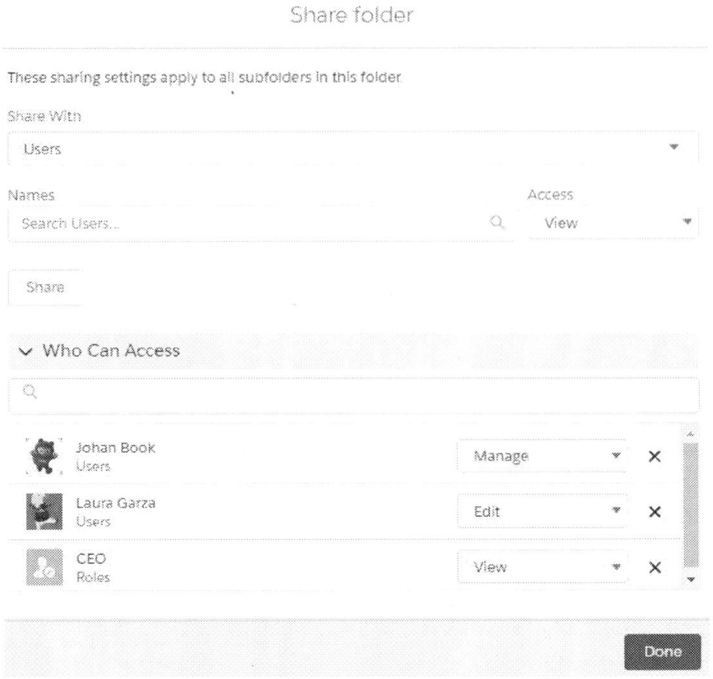

Figure 5.6 – Sharing Report Folder created

10. Because you are the one who created the EMEA Sales folder, this will appear under **Created by Me** under the Folders panel, also under All Folders. While for Laura Garza as in *Figure 5.6*, the `EMEA Sales` folder will appear under **Shared with Me** and **All Folders**.

> **Notes**
>
> If you do not have access to a folder, it will not appear under your **All Folders** menu.

In the exercise above, you learned how to create a report folder and add users to access the folders with different types of accessibility. As mentioned, the **report folder controls users' access to the reports** in that folder, **not on the report itself**.

> **Notes**
>
> If you do not have access to a folder, it will not appear under your **All Folders** menu.

Using Subfolders

Another feature available when storing reports is subfolders. With subfolders, you can more clearly organize the storage of your reports. For example, you can create multiple subfolders under EMEA Sales, such as Germany Sales, France Sales, etc., so the local teams know exactly which reports are applicable to them.

Now, let's continue our hands-on challenge to create subfolders under EMEA Sales

1. Open the **EMEA Sales** report folder. Notice you will see EMEA Sales under **All Folders** or **Created by Me** (for report folder created by you)

Figure 5.7 – Opening a Report Folder

2. Click the **New Folder** button, you need to make sure that you are under the right folder, e.g., EMEA Sales before clicking the button, otherwise, it will become a folder or subfolder of other folders.
3. Type `Germany Sales` in **Folder Label**, then click Folder Unique Name textbox, the value will be auto populated.
4. Click the **Save** button, now you should see the Germany Sales subfolder under the EMEA Sales folder.

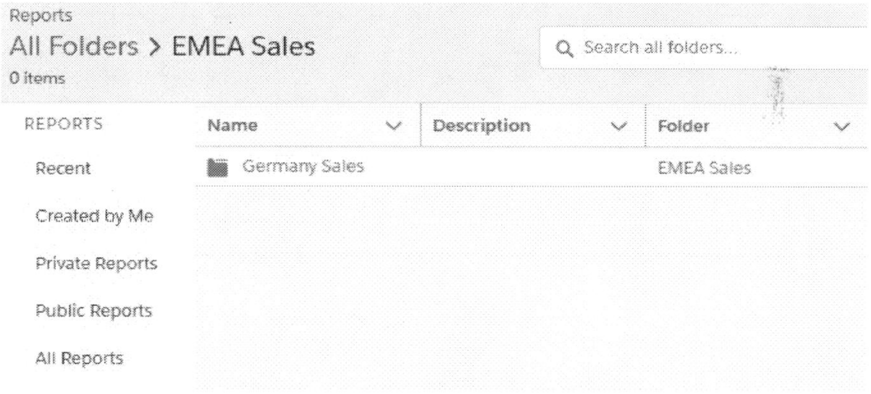

Figure 5.8 – The subfolder created

5. If you click the arrow at the further right of the subfolder, you will not see the Share menu, but the **View Share** menu, this is because access to the subfolder is following the main parent Folder access.

You can follow the same exercise to create subfolders under a subfolder for up to **3-levels**.

Notes

Please note that although subfolders can be used to organize/manage reports, the access permissions are inherited by the parent folder and cannot be different.

So now you have learned about multiple types of report folders, from the public, private, and shared folders. In the shared folders, you can set the report visibility and accessibility for each user. You can also make use of subfolders to organize reports practically and efficiently and give access to subfolders that will follow the parent folder sharing access.

Building Report Types

Another important item to consider when building your report besides report folders is **report type** which you can consider as a **template** to make your report building easier. There are two important concepts to decide on related to report type:

1. Fields available for reporting
2. Report result

When creating a report from scratch, always the first step is to select a report type. Report type plays an important role in building a report and this needs to be selected carefully, because you cannot change the report type once the report has been created.

It is based on the relationships between a primary object and its related objects. Reports display only records that meet the criteria defined in the report type.

Standard & Custom Report Types

There are two main types of report types:

1. Standard report type
2. Custom report type

The differences are shown in *Table 5.1*

Standard Report Type	**Custom Report Type**
Provided by Salesforce	Created and deployed by someone in your organization
All fields in the related objects available in the report type	Fields available on the report type chosen by the report type creator
Cannot be updated and deleted	Can be updated and deleted

Table 5.1 – Standard versus Custom report type

Salesforce provides a set of predefined standard report types based on the objects you have available, such as Accounts, Opportunities with Contact Roles, Campaign with Contacts, and so on, including from custom objects. For standard report types, one thing to note from the report type name is the word "**with**".

For example, if you use report type = Opportunities with Contact Roles, the report result will be all **Opportunities with at least one Contact Roles**, so Opportunities without any Contact Roles will not be in the report result. So, this explains that **report type impacts the report result**. Side note, in *Chapter 6, Advanced Reporting Features,* we will learn about **Cross Filter** where we can manually filter only records with or without child records.

You will find that most report types are available out of the box or created by Salesforce admins or other consultants. However, you can be given access to create custom report types if you have **Manage Custom Report Types** permission. The report type name depends on the report type creator.

> **Best practice**
>
> Always set a clear report type name, including what content that report type is representing.

The good thing about standard report types is those report types will have all the fields you need available from that object. For example, when your Salesforce admin creates new custom fields in the Opportunity object:

- For a standard report type, the new fields created will be available by default (only if you have access to the field)
- For custom report type, the new custom field will not be available by default, unless your admin enables **Auto-add to custom report type** when creating the new custom fields, or manually add the new fields in a particular report type.

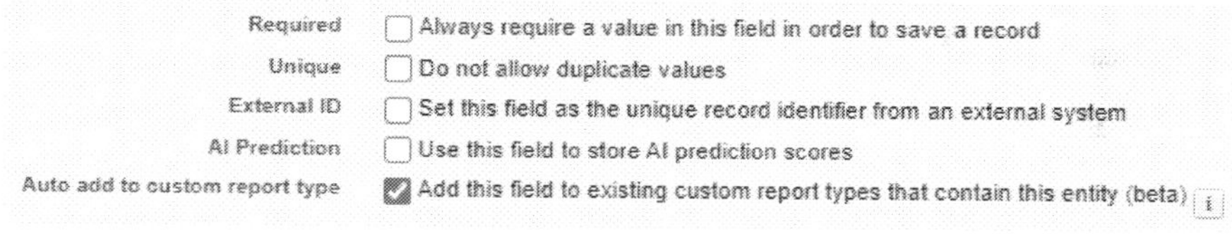

Figure 5.9 – Option to auto add a new custom field to the existing custom report types

As you see from the above bullet points, **report type determines fields availability** when creating or editing a report.

How to identify a Report Type

You will not be able to differentiate between a standard or custom report type when you select it on report creation. You will need to go to the Setup menu and search for Report Types, if you see the report type name exists, that means it is a custom report type, otherwise, it is a standard report type.

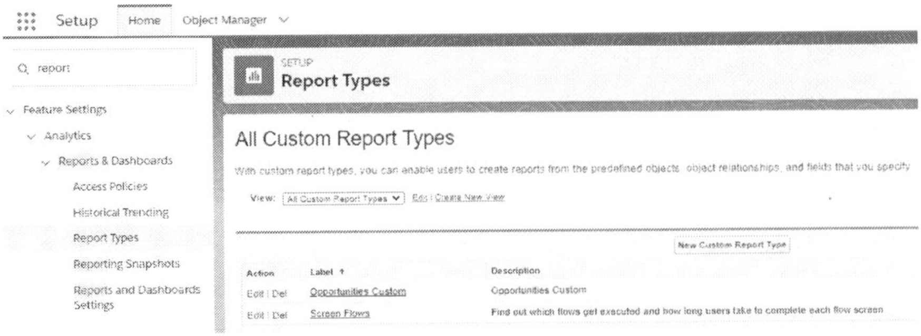

Figure 5.10 – Checking for custom report types

From here, we learned that report type plays a very important role in the building of a report, both standard and custom. Every report created will use one report type, which is the foundation of a report.

> **Tips**
>
> Before building your report, consider writing down each of the questions your report must answer. This way, your report is sure to return all the data you need.

Creating a Report from scratch

To be able to create and edit a report, you need to be granted **Create and Customize Reports** permission. If you are unable to follow the below due to this, reach out to your Salesforce admin.

As a start, you need to get to the **Report** tab where you will find the report builder. The report builder is a visual, drag-and-drop tool that you use to create reports and edit existing ones. When you create or edit a report, you choose which fields you want to include in your report in the report builder, including apply grouping, filtering, formula, and so on in the report builder.

To ensure your reports run quickly, it's a good idea to include only the fields that you need. Limit the data that your report returns by using filters. Filters are useful for many reasons, such as focusing your report on specific data, or ensuring that your report runs quickly. You can add, edit, or remove filters while reading a report too, as long as it is not locked from you to edit it.

Let's get hands-on to create a report called Open Opportunity:

1. Click the **Reports** tab
2. To launch the report builder, click **New Report.**
3. Select Opportunities from Choose Report Type window

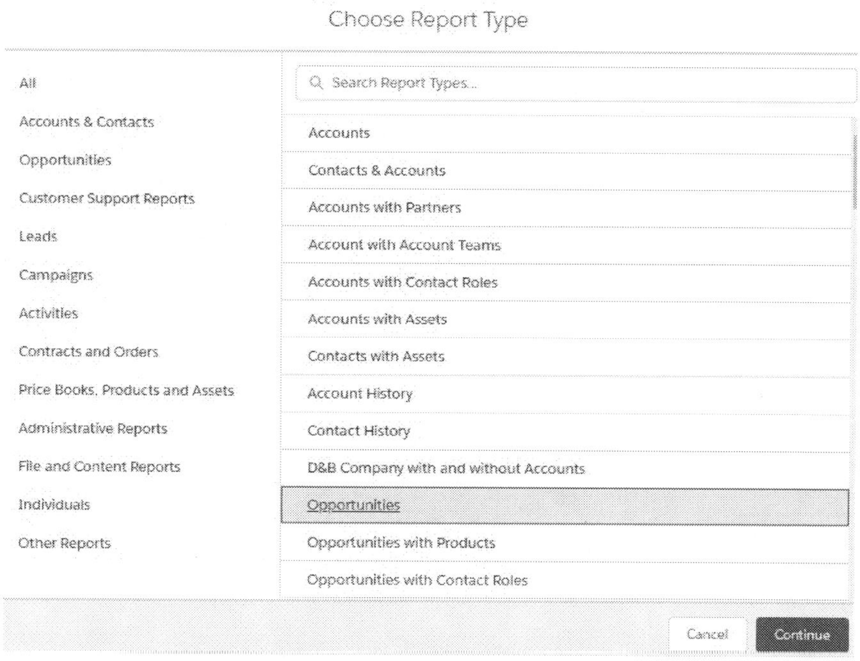

Figure 5.11 – Select a report type

4. Click the **Continue** button
5. Click the **Filters** tab, and select `Opportunity Status = Open`, then `Close Date = All Time`
6. Click **Apply** button
7. Click the **Outline** tab
8. To remove all default columns, click the arrow icon after **Columns** and select **Remove All Columns**

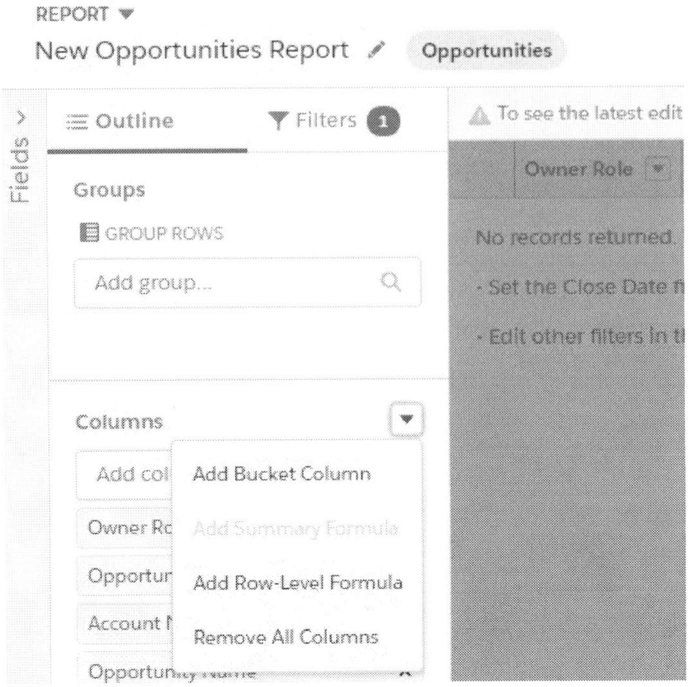

Figure 5.12 – Remove all default columns

9. Add the following column by type in the Add column… box
   - Opportunity Name
   - Stage
   - # Amount
   - Close Date
10. Click the **Save & Run** button
11. Here you can enter the report name and where to store the report, change the report name to `Open Opportunities`, and leave the Folder to **Private Reports**

Figure 5.13 – Saving a report

12. Click the **Save** button

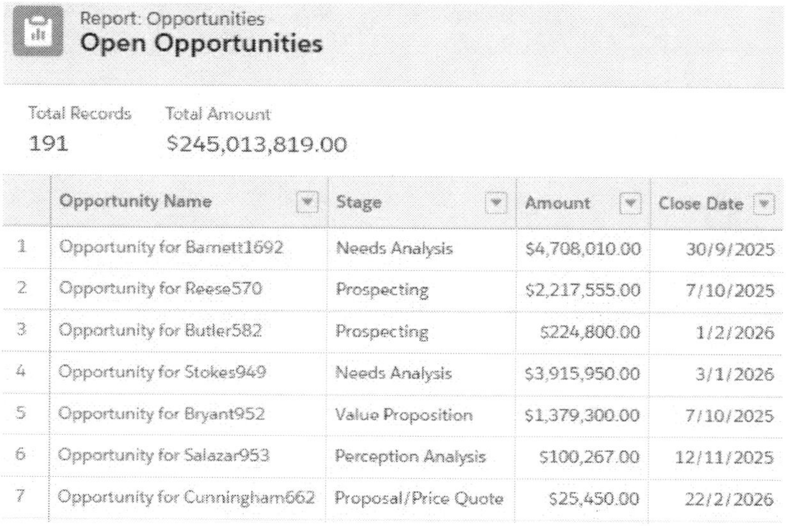

Figure 5.14 – Report created

Few things to note from *Figure 5.14*

- The report type name is shown above the report name, which is Opportunities
- You can click the header name to sort the report by the column as ascending or descending
- You also can click the arrow next to the column header to sort the report by the column ascending or descending, group the report by that column, or remove the column from the report.

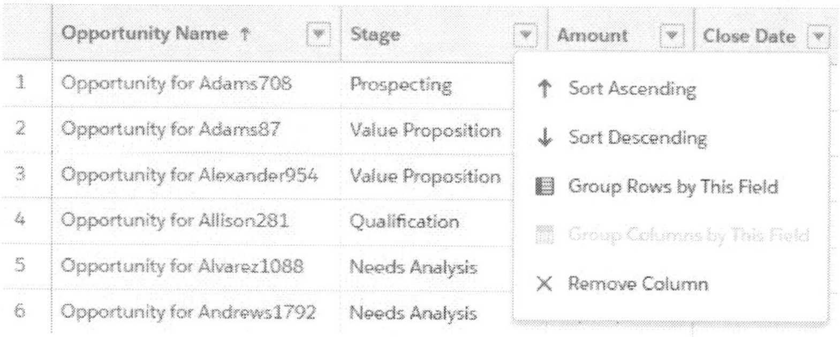

Figure 5.15 – Available options from report column

13. Click the **Groups Rows by This Field**
14. Deselect Details Rows at the report footer

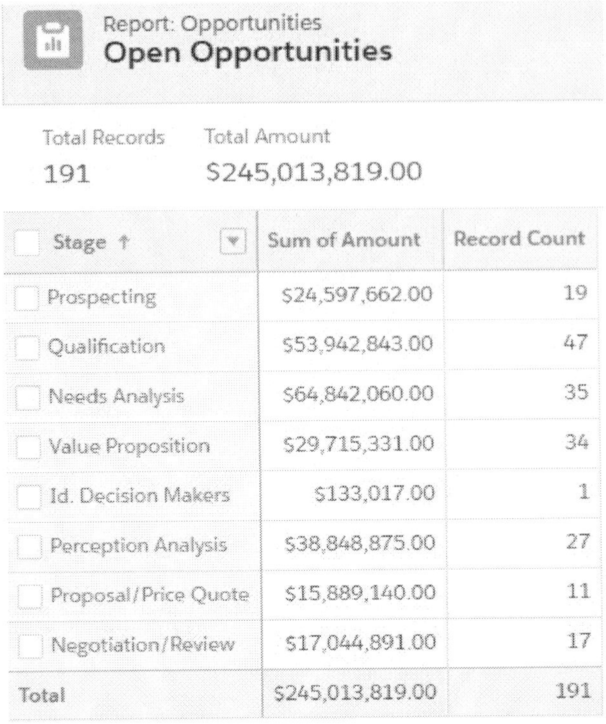
Report: Opportunities
Open Opportunities

Total Records 191
Total Amount $245,013,819.00

Stage ↑	Sum of Amount	Record Count
Prospecting	$24,597,662.00	19
Qualification	$53,942,843.00	47
Needs Analysis	$64,842,060.00	35
Value Proposition	$29,715,331.00	34
Id. Decision Makers	$133,017.00	1
Perception Analysis	$38,848,875.00	27
Proposal/Price Quote	$15,889,140.00	11
Negotiation/Review	$17,044,891.00	17
Total	$245,013,819.00	191

Figure 5.16 – Open Opportunities report by Stage

15. Now, we have open Opportunities report group by Stage

Editing Report

Similar to creating reports, you need to have with **Create and Customize Reports** permission to edit reports. When your report folder access is View, you will be able to run the report, edit the report, but unable to overwrite the report, you will be able to store the modified report in your Private folder, the Public folder, so Shared folders where you have Edit or Manage access.

Editing a report is the same as creating a report, but instead of building from scratch, editing a report gives you the report type, fields, formula, grouping, filters, etc. that have been built. Remember that you cannot change the report type of an existing report, while all other settings are modifiable.

Let's get hands-on to edit the Open Opportunities report created earlier. We are going to add groupings to the report column by Calendar Year of Close Date.

1. Open the Open Opportunities report
2. Click the **Edit** button
3. Enable **Details Rows** at the report footer
4. Click the arrow next to **Close Date** and select **Group Columns by This Field**

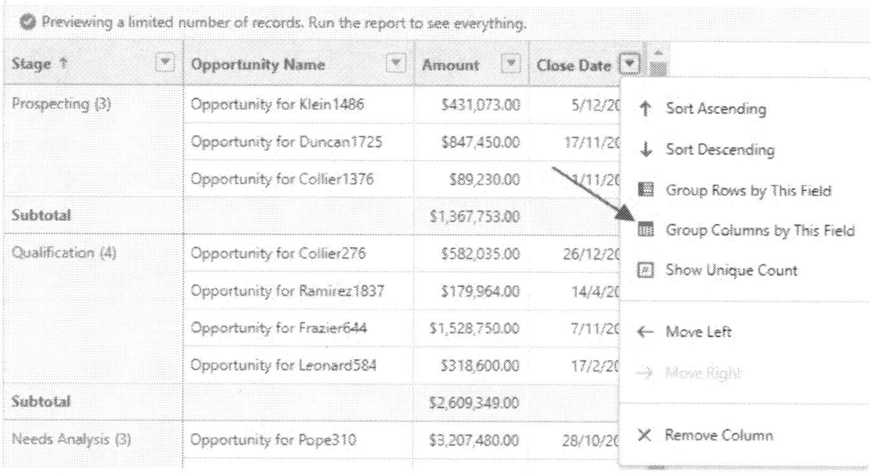

Figure 5.17 – Adding group column by Close Date

5. Make sure **Update Preview Automatically** at the far right below the Run button is enabled, if this option is not enabled, enable it now, so the report preview is updated
6. Now you should see a lot of columns by date, we are going to group this by Calendar Year, click the arrow next to **Close Date** and select **Group Date By ...** then **Calendar Year**

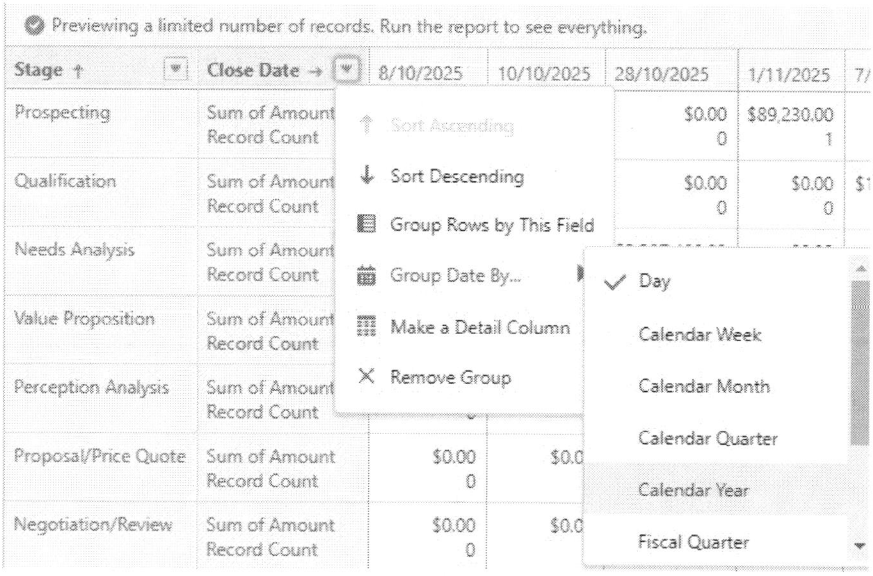

Figure 5.18 – Group Close Date by Calendar Year

7. Let us deselect Row Counts from the report footer
8. Click the Save & Run button

9. Now the report is grouped by Stage as rows, and group by Calendar Year of Closed Date by columns, see *Figure 5.19*, but your data will be different from mine.

Report: Opportunities
Open Opportunities

Total Amount
$245,013,819.00

Stage ↑	Close Date →	CY2021	CY2025	CY2026	Total
Prospecting	Sum of Amount	$0.00	$15,650,702.00	$8,946,960.00	$24,597,662.00
Qualification	Sum of Amount	$0.00	$24,868,237.00	$29,074,606.00	$53,942,843.00
Needs Analysis	Sum of Amount	$2,868,400.00	$36,057,010.00	$25,916,650.00	$64,842,060.00
Value Proposition	Sum of Amount	$0.00	$20,584,468.00	$9,130,863.00	$29,715,331.00
Id. Decision Makers	Sum of Amount	$0.00	$133,017.00	$0.00	$133,017.00
Perception Analysis	Sum of Amount	$0.00	$23,319,029.00	$15,529,846.00	$38,848,875.00
Proposal/Price Quote	Sum of Amount	$0.00	$13,372,790.00	$2,516,350.00	$15,889,140.00
Negotiation/Review	Sum of Amount	$0.00	$12,195,350.00	$4,849,541.00	$17,044,891.00
Total	Sum of Amount	$2,868,400.00	$146,180,603.00	$95,964,816.00	$245,013,819.00

Figure 5.19 – Open Opportunities group by Stage and Calendar Year of Close Date

After adding a group, you can show or hide Row Counts, Detail Rows, Subtotals, and Grand Total by clicking the switches at the bottom of the report.

Adding a Chart

An image tells a thousand words and the same applies to a chart as well. Once the report is created, you can easily add a chart. Let's add a chart to the Open Opportunities report created earlier.

1. Open the Open Opportunities report
2. Click **Add Chart** button on the upper right of the report. You will get a bar chart instantly added above the report table

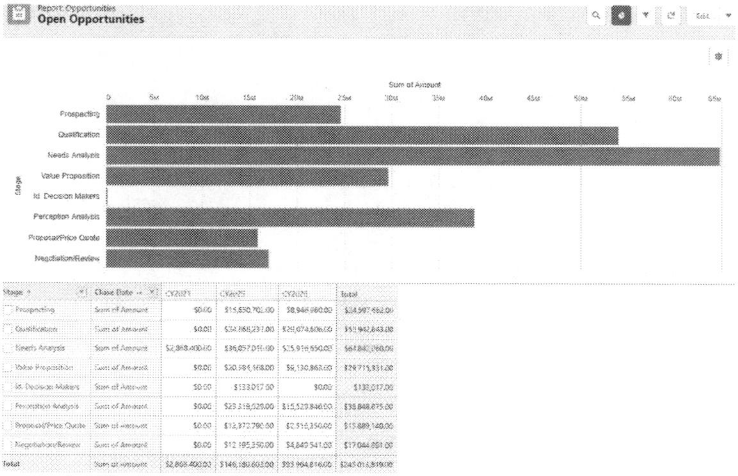

Figure 5.20 – Chart added to the report

3. Click the **gear icon** below the Edit button

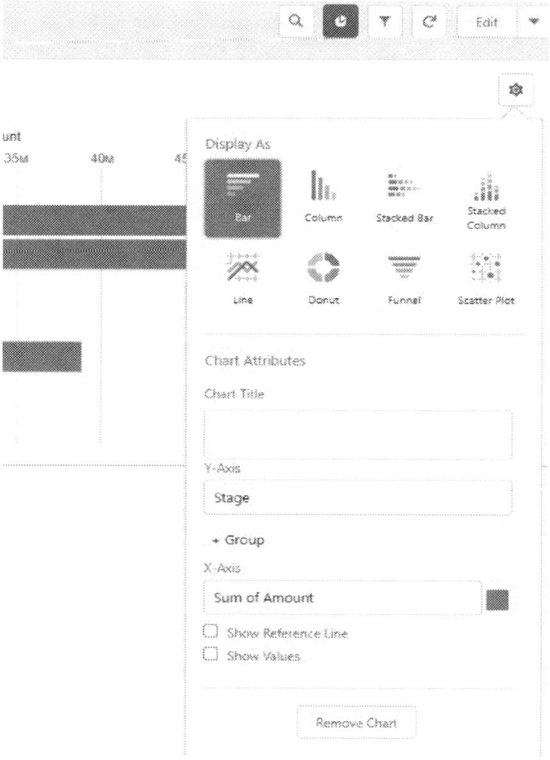

Figure 5.21 – Chart options

4. From this panel, you can modify the chart type, Title, and so on, the attributes are available based on the selected chart type. If you wish, you could also remove the chart from here.

5. I am going to change to a Donut chart and select **Show Value** and **Show Percentage**

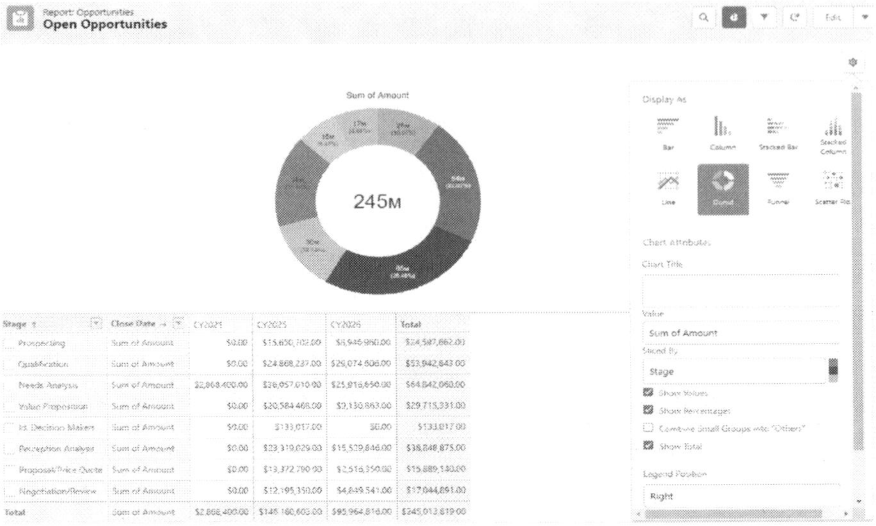

Figure 5.22 – Change to Donut chart

6. Click the **Save** button to save the chart. If you do not see this button, click the arrow next to the Edit button.

You have learned how to create a report by selecting a report type, how to add and remove filters or columns, how to group fields by rows or by columns, and how to edit an existing report, as well as add a chart. Next, we will learn another type of report called a Joined Report.

Useful Reporting Tips and Notes

- The preview pane shows a max of 20 records for summary or 50 for tabular reports. You need to run your report to see more records (up to 2000 records) and export the report to see all if there are more than 2000 records.
- Separate filter terms by commas to filter by more than one value. For example, to filter for accounts in California, New York, or Washington, use State contains CA, NY, WA.
- For exact match use 'Equals' but you can use 'contains' to include more results.
- When filtering on multi-select picklist fields, use a semicolon between values to specify an exact match. For example, selecting the "equals" operator and a semicolon between two values includes records with both values specified, excluding all other values. Also, make use of the "includes" and "excludes" operators when filtering a multi-select picklist field.
- Filtering isn't case-sensitive. For example, searching State contains ID returns all matches for "ID", but also returns any instances of "Florida" and "Idaho" because they contain "id" in their names.

- When you filter on standard long text area fields, such as Description, only the first 1000 characters of the field are searched for matches in reports.
- To filter to see blank values, just leave it blank on value selection, or pick from the "No Selection" value on the bottom of a picklist field
- Always check to see if a report exists you can use or clone before building your own.
- Once your report is run, always check a couple of the results to ensure it is what you expect. If it is missing anything or has something that should not be there, use those records to check against your filters. There is almost always a logical reason.
- To ensure you are getting the data you think you need, pull the filter fields into the report also to double-check. You can always remove them after view/export.
- Make use of Relative dates such as TODAY, THIS FISCAL YEAR, n MONTHS AGO, etc. for the complete list, check out this article *https://help.salesforce.com/articleView?id=sf.filter_dates_relative.htm&type=5*
- A Lead report pulls converted leads information, to remove those already converted, use filter Converted equals False.
- You can search reports in the Global Search bar.
- Use favorites to save reports you often run. You can even add them to your navigation bar after this.
- Delete reports you no longer use.

Introducing the Joined Report

Joined Reports are a report that combines data from multiple reports (or multiple Objects) into blocks. All blocks should have a common field to group those reports. For example, you want to see Open Opportunities and Open Cases of customers, but you cannot create that kind of report in Salesforce without using a Joined Report.

Let's get hands-on to experience Joined Reports:

1. Click the **Reports** tab, then click the **New Report** button
2. Select report type Opportunities
3. Click in Filters tab and change Close Date = All Time, and Opportunity Status = Open
4. Click the Outline tab, and select Remove All Columns from the arrow next to the Column
5. Add the following fields: Opportunity Name, Stage, and Amount
6. Click Report on the upper left corner, and select Joined Report then click the Apply button

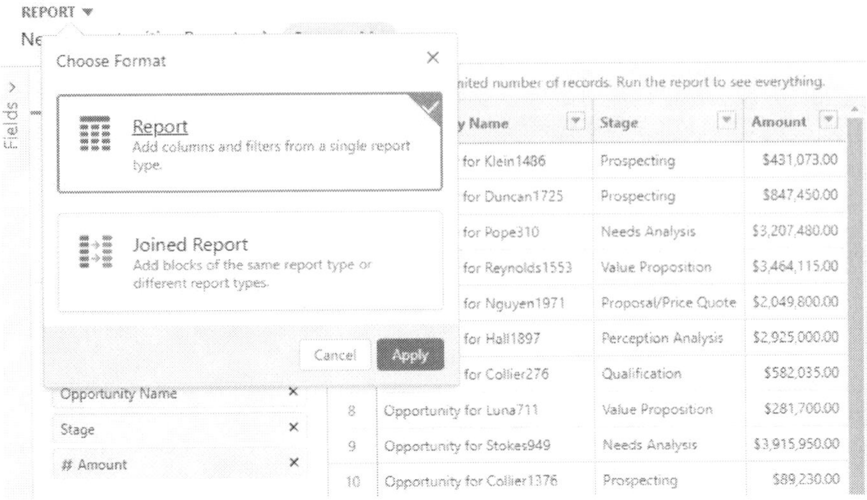

Figure 5.23 – Change to Joined Report

7. Click the **Add Block** button next to the report name
8. Select report type `Cases`, deselect to Include default columns, then click Add Block button
9. Add the following fields under Cases block 1: Case Number, Subject, Status
10. Click the **Filters** tab, under Cases block 1, add filter Closed = False
11. Back to the **Outlines** tab, under Groups Across Blocks, select Account Name

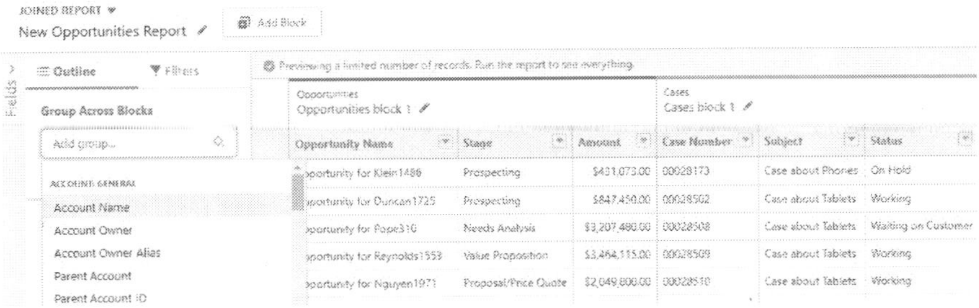

Figure 5.24 – Add field to Group Across Blocks

12. Deselect **Subtotals** at the report footer
13. Click **Save & Run** button
14. Change the Report Name to **Account with Open Opportunities & Cases**, click the Save button

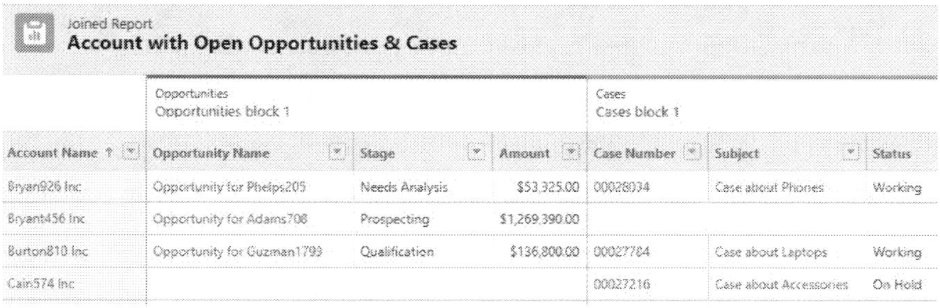

Joined Report
Account with Open Opportunities & Cases

	Opportunities Opportunities block 1			Cases Cases block 1		
Account Name ↑	Opportunity Name	Stage	Amount	Case Number	Subject	Status
Bryan926 Inc	Opportunity for Phelps205	Needs Analysis	$53,325.00	00028034	Case about Phones	Working
Bryant456 Inc	Opportunity for Adams708	Prospecting	$1,269,390.00			
Burton810 Inc	Opportunity for Guzman1799	Qualification	$136,800.00	00027784	Case about Laptops	Working
Cain574 Inc				00027216	Case about Accessories	On Hold

Figure 5.25 – A Joined Report

From *Figure 5.25*, notice that if there is no data for a block (Opportunities block 1 or Case block 1), it will just be blank. Once the report is created, you can do the following:

- Add Chart
- Click the Filter icon to change the filters for both blocks if needed
- Change "Opportunities block 1" and "Cases block 1" to something more meaningful, such as `Open Opportunities` and `Open Cases`, you need to edit the report to perform this

Here are the updated reports:

	Opportunities Open Opportunities			Cases Open Cases		
Account Name ↑	Opportunity Name	Stage	Amount	Case Number	Subject	Status
Acme USA				00027783	Case about Laptops	Waiting on Customer
Adkins907 Inc	Opportunity for Morton591	Proposal/Price Quote	$1,741,100.00			
Aguilar870 Inc	Opportunity for Parker1715	Negotiation/Review	$886,570.00			
	Opportunity for Evans911	Value Proposition	$185,630.00			
Alexander704 Inc				00027844	Case about Laptops	Working

Figure 5.26 – Updated Joined Report

Notes

Joined Reports offers a different type of reporting, each block ideally using different report types, but has common fields across all blocks for grouping purposes. In some use cases, you can use the same report type across blocks.

Inline Editing in a Report

Inline Editing in a report is a new feature introduced as Beta in Summer '21 release (June 2021). With inline editing, you can edit the data directly inside a report. Not all fields can be edited from the report, such as:

- Owner field
- Record Type field

Before you can use this feature, your Salesforce Admin needs to activate it from the Setup menu by searching for **Reports and Dashboards Settings**, select **Enable Inline Editing in Reports** (Lightning Experience only) and Save.

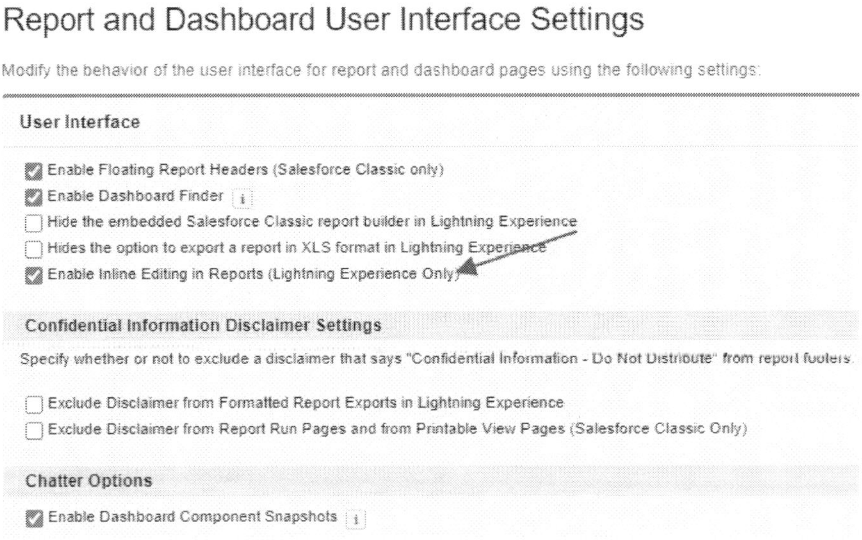

Figure 5.27 – Admin need to enable Inline Editing from Setup

Once this feature is enabled, all users will be able to edit fields as long as the user has edit access to the record and the fields. Also, inline editing respects permission in the page layout, so if the user is unable to edit a field on the record page, the user will be not able to use inline editing either

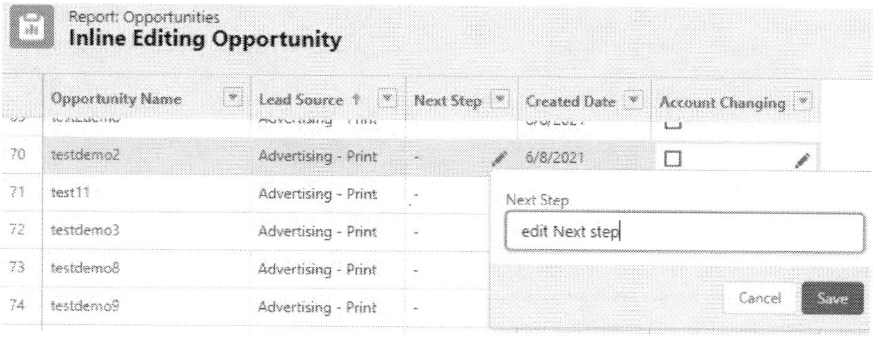

Figure 5.28 – Use Inline Editing to update fields from a report

Summary

This chapter introduces you to the reporting functionality in Salesforce, which is one of the most powerful features loved by many Salesforce users, no matter your level or role. You can examine your Salesforce data in almost infinite combinations, display it in easy-to-understand formats, and share the resulting insights with others. The report access is controlled by the report folders it is stored in, and not by the report itself.

Here are a few best practices related to reporting:

- Always store reports in a folder based on the required access. So, keep reports in your Private folder if you do not want them to be visible to other users
- Only give Edit and Manage permission in the report folder for users that need to edit or share reports
- Make use of subfolders to organize shared reports
- Select the right report type when creating a report, as you cannot change the report type once selected. The type also impacts the report result and the fields available when building your report
- Remove unnecessary fields from a report as they will slow down your report

We are just beginning to introduce all the available reporting module features available to you, Salesforce reporting has so many features we don't want you to miss, so in the next *Chapter 6, Advanced Reporting*, we will discuss using more advanced features, such as summary formulas, cross filters, etc. so keep reading and following to learn more!

CHAPTER 6:

ADVANCED REPORTING FEATURES

In *Chapter 5*, *Reporting on the Cloud*, we learned the foundations of Salesforce reporting, from choosing the correct report type, to accessing and sharing reports using folders and subfolders, to creating, editing, and adding charts to a report, to using joined reports, and finally, using inline editing. If you have not read Chapter 5, I would suggest reading it first to learn the basics.

In this chapter, we will learn advanced features of Salesforce reporting, including these topics:

- Filter Logic
- Cross Filter
- Drill Down
- Report Parameter
- Unique Count
- Bucket Column
- Row-Level Formula
- Summary Formula
- Subscriptions
- Adding Reports to a Dashboard
- Export Report

Filter Logic

When we run a report, usually we only want to see a specific portion of the data. We can do so by adding one or more filters to our report, which has been discussed in *Chapter 5*. If you add more than one filter, the relation of all fields by default is **AND**.

Using Filter Logic, we can define the relationship across filters with **AND** and **OR** logic, by making use of brackets () to set the order of operation.

Let us now get hands-on with filter logic. In this scenario, I would like to see all customers (Accounts) in Germany and Italy, and also customers (Accounts) in Belgium, but only for the Retail industry.

1. Create a new report, from the **Reports** tab
2. Choose report type = **Accounts**
3. Remove all default fields, then add these fields we would like to see `Account Name`, `Account Owner`, `Type`, `Industry`, `Billing Country`
4. In the Filters tab, make sure to select **All accounts** and Created Date = `All Time`
5. Add the following filters
    a. Billing Country = `Germany, Italy`
    b. Billing Country = `Belgium`
    c. Industry = `Retail`
6. Do not worry if the report shows no data yet, this is because filters 5a plus 5b will produce no data, remember the default logic is AND
7. Add Filter Logic by click the arrow icon next to Filters, then select **Add Filter Logic**

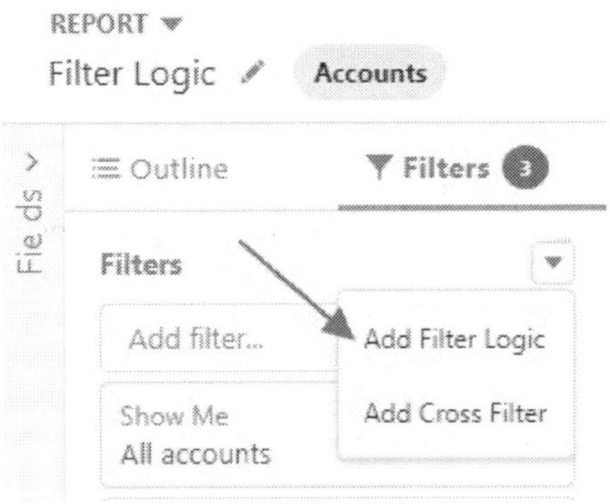

Figure 6.1 – Adding Filter Logic

8. Change the default filter logic from 1 AND 2 AND 3 to `1 OR (2 AND 3)` then click the **Apply** button.

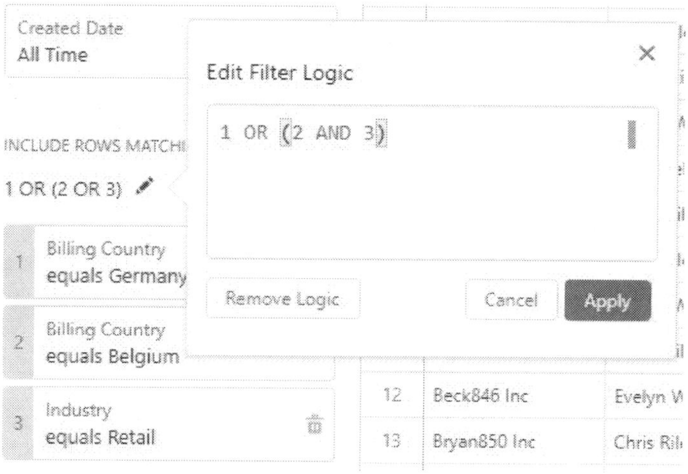

Figure 6.2 – Edit Filter Logic values

9. Done! The report now contains filter logic with the results you are after, and you can now save the report to a folder for future reference

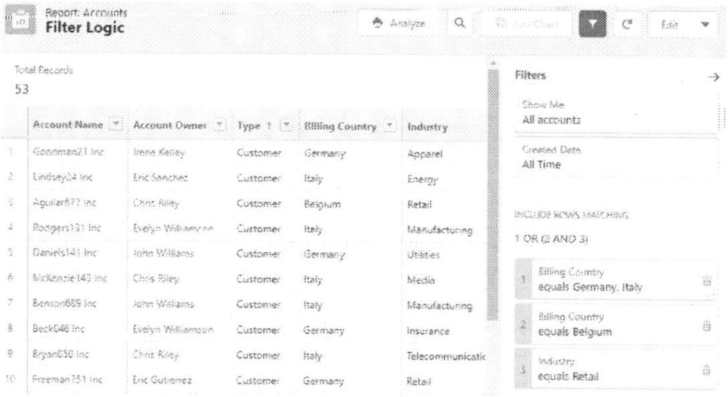

Figure 6.3 – Running a report with filter Logic

From the above exercise, we made use of the comma to filter a field with multiple values and we also made use of brackets to set the order of filter logic, as you can see here, as each number represents a field added as a filter.

> **Tips**
>
> If you need to filter a field with many values, you do not need to add the same field multiple times then use OR logic, but simply just add a comma between values.

Cross Filter

The cross filter allows you to extend your reports to objects related to the primary object defined in the report type, such as the relation to its child object. The most common use case is exception reporting, such as **Accounts without Opportunities**, but you could also do **Accounts with Opportunities**, **Accounts with Open Opportunities**, etc., this report is useful when you need to analyze data and gain further insights.

The information available on the cross filter is determined by your report type selected.

Let's see how this works in an example below, where we would like to use Filter Logic to show Accounts with Open Opportunities only:

1. Open the Filter Logic report from the previous hands-on exercise and click the **Edit** button
2. Click **Filters** tab, click the arrow icon next to **Filters**, then select **Add Cross Filter**

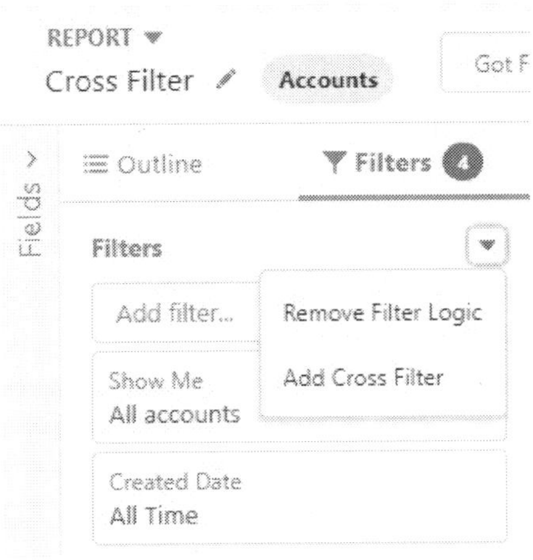

Figure 6.4 – Adding Cross Filter

3. In the Secondary Object, select **Opportunities** then click **Apply** button, keep the **with** value

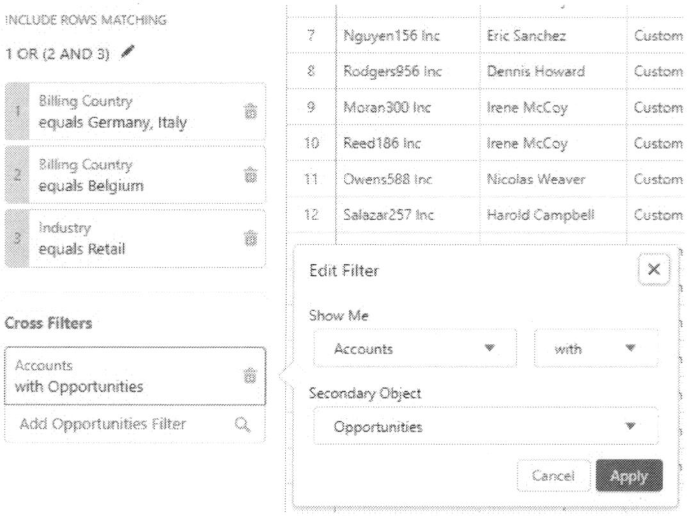

Figure 6.5 – Adding Cross Filter with Secondary Object

4. Now we have the cross filter added as Accounts with Opportunities, but we want to see only Accounts with **Open** Opportunities. So, let us continue, in **Add Opportunities Filter** textbox under **Cross Filters**, click that textbox and select **Closed** = **False**, then click the **Apply** button.

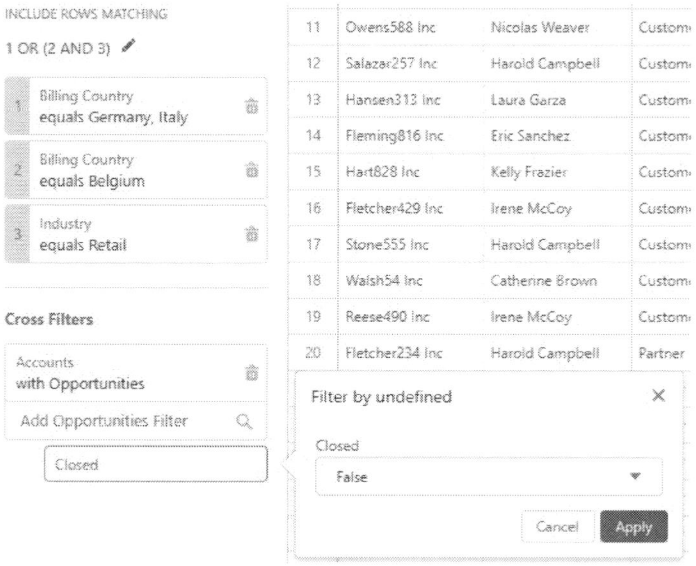

Figure 6.6 – Adding Filter under Cross Filter

5. Now, we are done, click the **Save As** from the arrow in the **Save** button, and enter a new report name. The final report in *Figure 6.7* will show only Accounts with at least one open Opportunity.

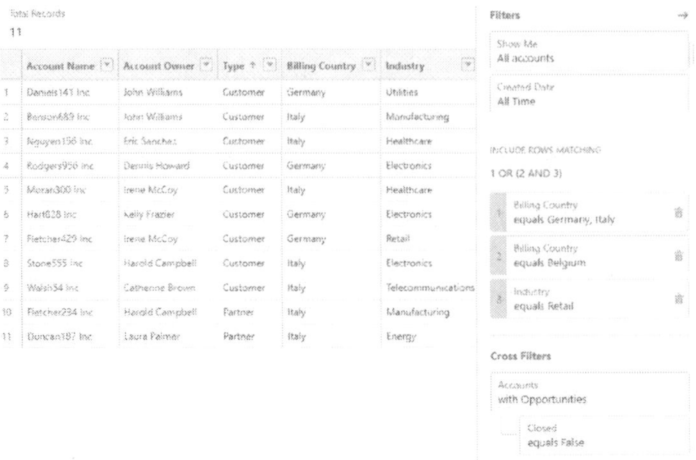

Figure 6.7 – Accounts with Open Opportunities report

Drill Down

When you need to perform data analysis in Salesforce, you may need to drill data into a specific dataset based on the report result, simply because you do not know the data yet, so cannot add those filters when creating the report. Drill down is useful when the report has too much data and you need to focus on a specific dataset only.

Salesforce reporting offers drill-down capabilities to filter the data based on your selection. The only requirement is, the report must have at least one **grouping**.

Let's get hands-on using the report created earlier in Filter Logic. We are going to drill down Account based on the Account Owner.

1. Open the Filter Logic report and click the **Edit** button
2. Drag `Account Owner` field from **Columns** to **Group Rows** panel

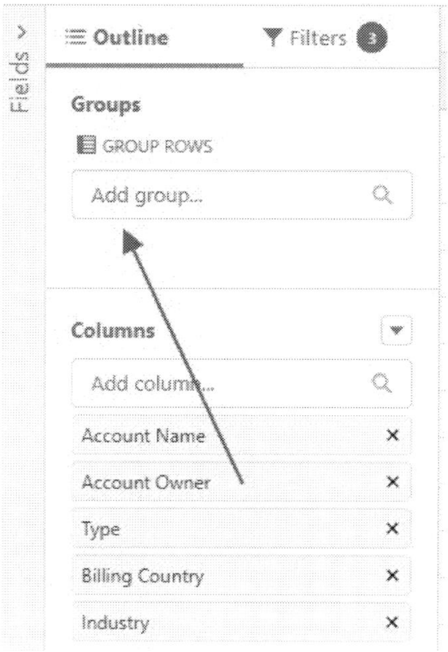

Figure 6.8 – Adding field for grouping

3. Deselect **Subtotals** from the report footer
4. Click the **Save As** from the arrow next to the Save button and enter a new report name.
5. Click the **Run** button to see the result, the report is now group by Account Owner as per *Figure 6.9*
6. To drill down data based on selected groups, click one or multiple checkboxes next to the group name, then click the **Drill Down** button. You must select the checkbox to see the **Drill Down button**, the button label will show how many groups are selected.

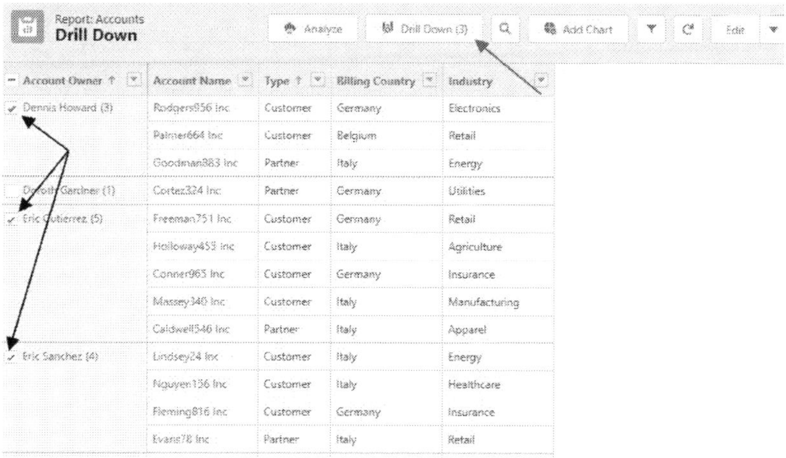

Figure 6.9 – Adding field for grouping

7. Click the **Drill Down** (x) button, by default, the system will offer you to use the current field grouping, but you can change to group by other fields, for now, let us keep the default field, group by **Account Owner** then click **Apply** button.

8. Now the report only shows the selected Account Owner, instead of all. If you click the **Filter** icon, notice that Account Owner is added as a filter with values of selected Account Owner.

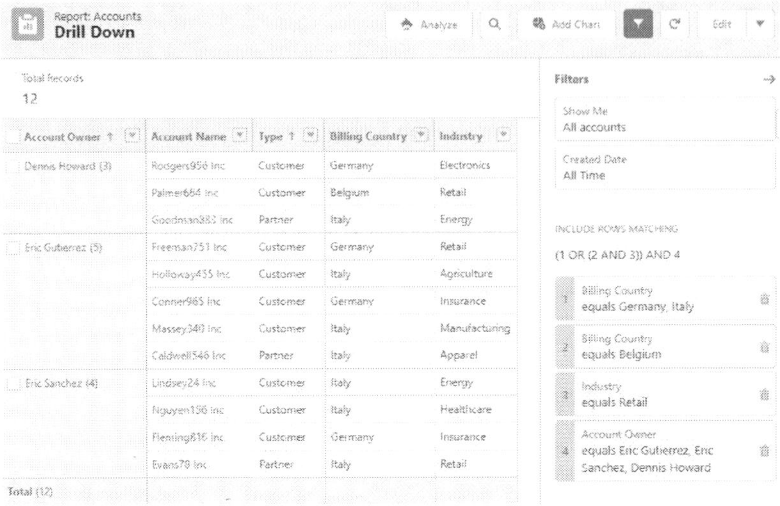

Figure 6.10 – Account Owner added as a filter after Drill down

9. Click the **Save** button again to store the changes.

If you ask, can I add the Account Owner manually as a filter? Of course you can, and the result will be the same as the result from drill down, but why do we need to use the Drill Down button instead? Because we do not know the values to filter when creating the report, so this is part of the data analysis process.

Report Parameters

We learned how to add filters in Chapter 5 whilst creating a report, it is pretty simple just by typing the field name and the values in the **Filters** tab. However, Salesforce reporting does not stop there. You can also update the filter value on the fly without editing the report. In a popular use case here, you can create one report for multiple teams, and each team will only see their own data.

A few things you need to note before implementing the report parameter:

- You need to learn URL in the web browser
- You need to know filters added to the report and count the order of the filters
- **fv0** as the 1st filter value, **fv1** as the 2nd filter value, and continue

Now, let's get hands-on by using the initial Filter Logic report. Again, we are going to change the filter values on the fly.

1. Open the Filter Logic report
2. Look at the report URL in the web browser, for example, mine is *https://bookcom3-dev-ed.lightning.force.com/lightning/r/Report/00O5g00000ARlLXEA1/view*
3. We are going to change the value of the first filter value, which is Billing Country, originally is `Germany, Italy` but we are going to change to `Spain`, you just need to add **?fv0=Spain** at the end of the original URL, so the final URL is *https://bookcom3-dev-ed.lightning.force.com/lightning/r/Report/00O5g00000ARlLXEA1/view?fv0=Spain*

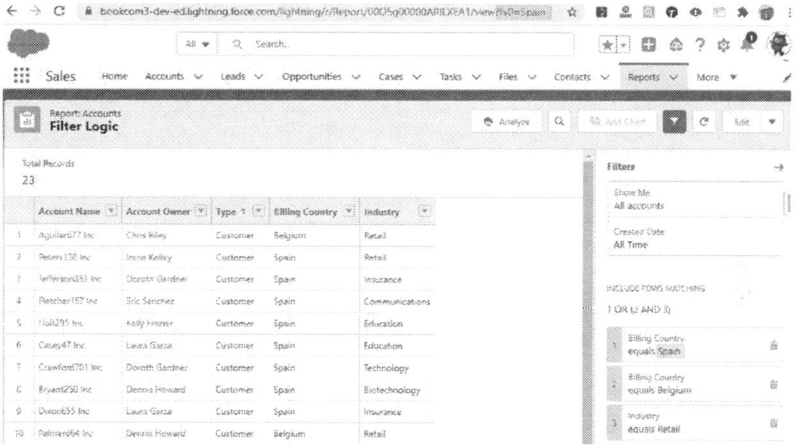

Figure 6.11 – Adding a parameter in the report URL for report filter

4. If you need to change more filter values, you can use **&** after the **1st filter**, example, I want to change the Industry from Retail to `Insurance` *https://bookcom3-dev-ed.lightning.force.com/lightning/r/Report/00O5g00000ARlLXEA1/view?fv0=Spain&fv2=Insurance*. Because Industry is the 3rd filter, so add **fv2** and remember to add **&** after the 1st parameter.

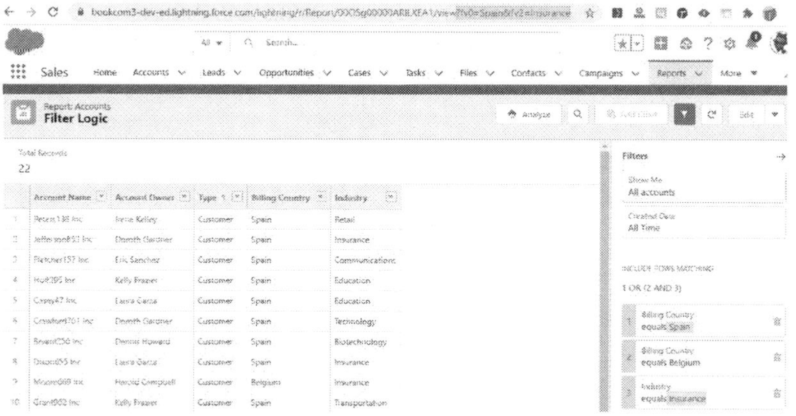

Figure 6.12 – Adding multiple parameters for report filter

5. If you open the original report, the filter values are not changed.

Unique Count

The purpose of Unique Count is to tell us how many **unique** records that show in a report, for a tabular report (without grouping), the count will be shown at the top of the report, while a report with a grouping will show in the subtotal and also at the top of the report.

Next, with our hands-on exercise, we will use the Drill Down report saved earlier to get a Unique Count.

1. Open the Drill Down report made earlier and click the **Edit** button
2. Delete your Filter for Account Owner
3. Click the arrow next to the Billing Country column, then select **Show Unique Count**

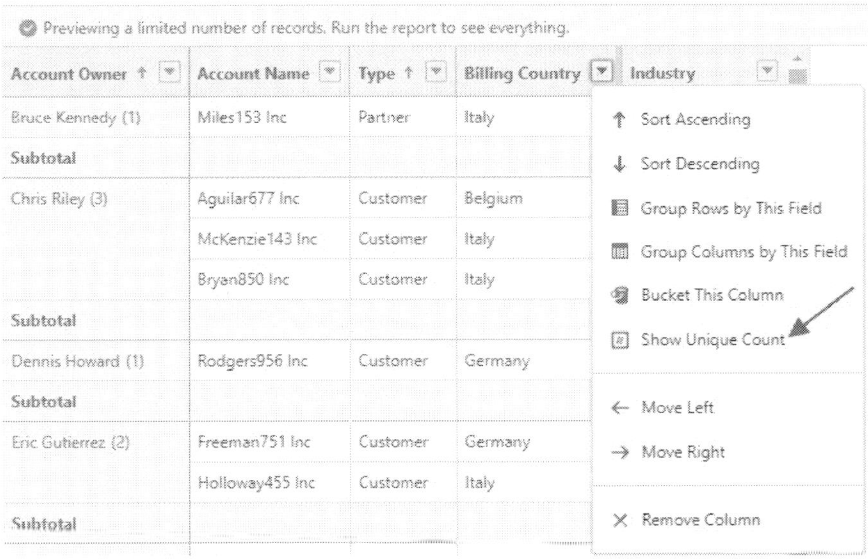

Figure 6.13 – Select Show Unique Count for a field

4. Click **Save As** from the arrow next to the Save button and enter a new report name.
5. Click the **Run** button to see the result. The report is now grouped by Account Owner as per *Figure 6.14*
6. Notice that Unique Count is added in the Subtotal and at the top of the report.

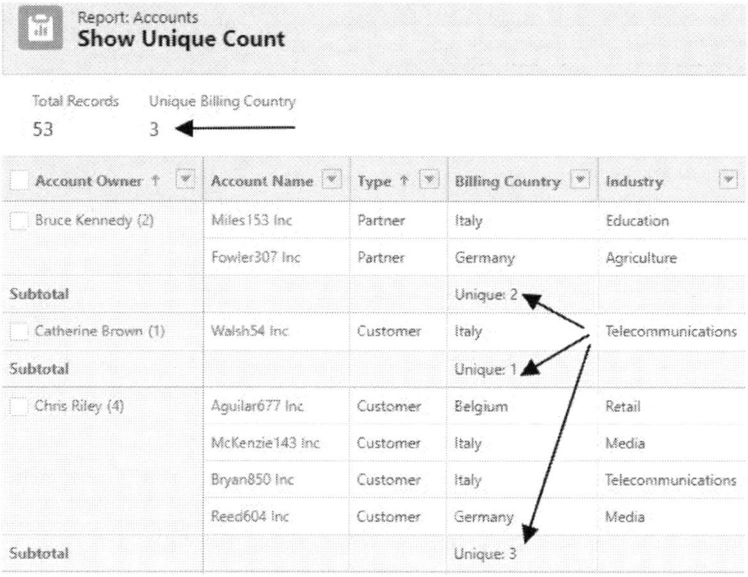

Report: Accounts
Show Unique Count

Total Records: 53
Unique Billing Country: 3

Account Owner	Account Name	Type	Billing Country	Industry
Bruce Kennedy (2)	Miles153 Inc	Partner	Italy	Education
	Fowler307 Inc	Partner	Germany	Agriculture
Subtotal			Unique: 2	
Catherine Brown (1)	Walsh54 Inc	Customer	Italy	Telecommunications
Subtotal			Unique: 1	
Chris Riley (4)	Aguilar677 Inc	Customer	Belgium	Retail
	McKenzie143 Inc	Customer	Italy	Media
	Bryan850 Inc	Customer	Italy	Telecommunications
	Reed604 Inc	Customer	Germany	Media
Subtotal			Unique: 3	

Figure 6.14 – Unique Count of a field in the report

Bucket Column

The purpose of the bucketing column is to combine a few values into a single value, for example, Italy, Spain, and Portugal can be bucketed as Southern Europe, while Germany, Belgium, Denmark can be bucketed as Northern Europe. The new value will be stored as a new field in that report. The added bucket column will only be available on that report and have no impact on other reports or the data.

Let's do a quick hands-on exercise re-using our Filter Logic report. We will bucket Italy, Spain, and Turkey as Southern Europe, whilst Germany, Belgium, Denmark will be bucketed as Northern Europe.

1. Open the Filter Logic report created earlier and click the **Edit** button
2. Delete All Filters in this report, and add filters for Billing Country = Italy, Spain, Turkey, Germany, Belgium, Denmark
3. Click the arrow next to the Billing Country and select **Bucket This Column**

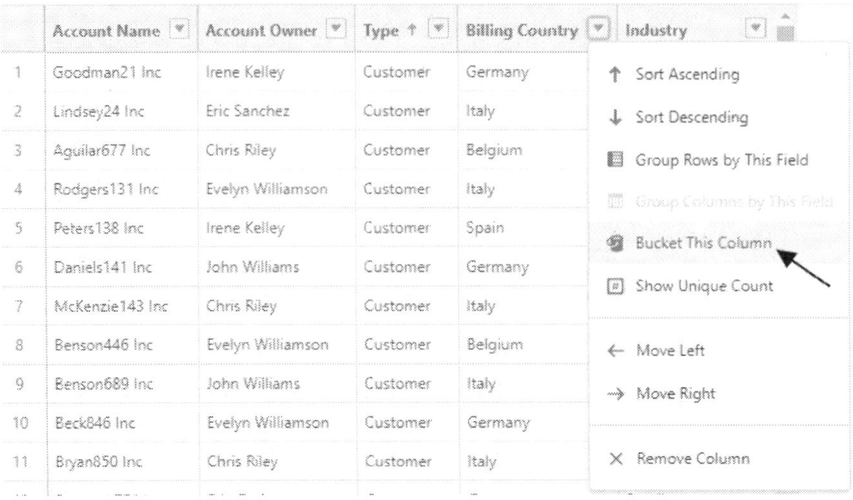

Figure 6.15 – Select Bucket Column of a field

4. On the bucket name, type `Europe`, in this case, Europe will become the column/field name, then click **Add Bucket** button, in the Bucket name, type `Southern Europe`
5. Click the **Unbucket Values** tab, then select `Italy`, `Spain`, and `Turkey` in the values and click **Move To** button, and select **Southern Europe**

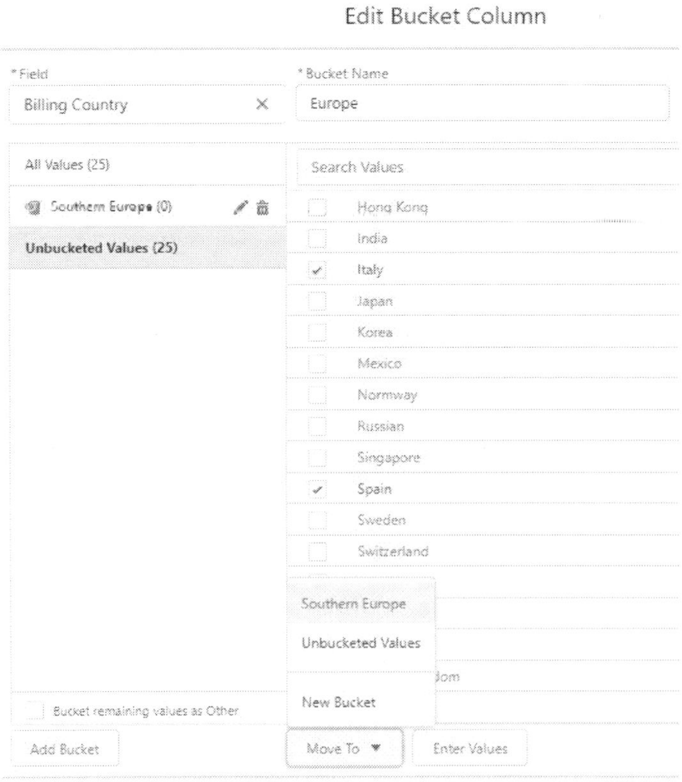

Figure 6.16 – Add Bucket and values

6. Repeat Step 5 for Northern Europe by adding `Germany`, `Belgium`, and `Denmark`
7. Click the **Apply** button, the **Run** the report
8. You can group the report with this new bucket field by clicking the arrow next to the column and select **Group Rows by This Field**

Figure 6.17 – Group Rows from a running report

9. Now your report should be grouped by the new bucket column.
10. Click the **Save As** from the arrow next to the Edit button and enter a new report name.

Row-Level Formula

The row-level formula allows you to use a formula field in your report, which will not exist in the database and on other reports. This is a new feature that is not available in the older Salesforce Classic, so you must use Lightning to use this feature and allows you to make use of temporary fields rather than having to have your Salesforce admin add extra fields likely unnecessary in the medium to long term.

Let's now get hands-on to use row-level formulas. In this scenario, we are going to create a row-level formula field to check if the Account has been updated since it was created.

1. Create a new report and select report type = **Accounts**
2. Remove all default fields, and add the following fields in the report: `Account Name`, `Created Date`, and `Last Modified Date`
3. Click the arrow icon next to Columns and select **Add Row-Level Formula**

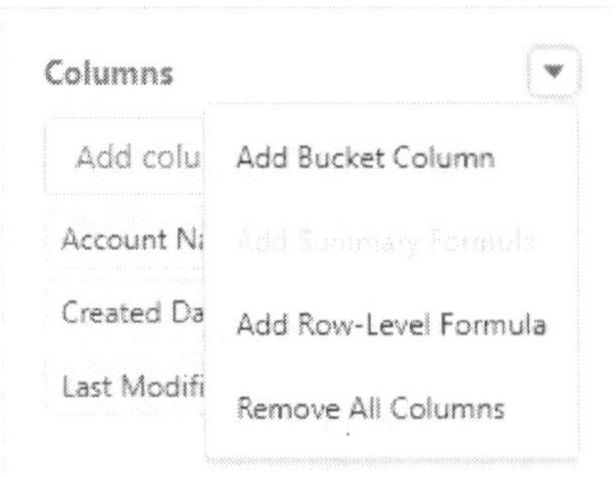

Figure 6.18 – Adding Row-Level Formula to report

4. In the row-level formula window, enter the following:
   - Column Name = `Never Update`
   - Formula Output Type = **Text**
   - Formula =

   `IF(CREATED_DATE = LAST_UPDATE,"True","False")`
5. Click the **Apply** button, then **Save & Run** button

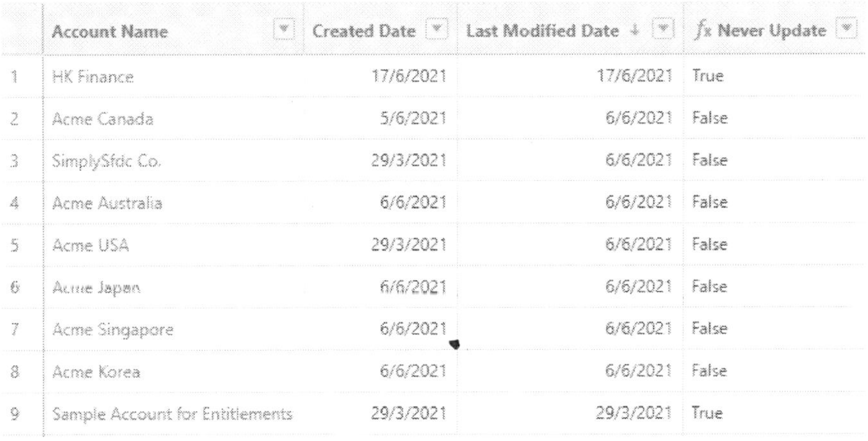

	Account Name	Created Date	Last Modified Date ↓	*fx* Never Update
1	HK Finance	17/6/2021	17/6/2021	True
2	Acme Canada	5/6/2021	6/6/2021	False
3	SimplySfdc Co.	29/3/2021	6/6/2021	False
4	Acme Australia	6/6/2021	6/6/2021	False
5	Acme USA	29/3/2021	6/6/2021	False
6	Acme Japan	6/6/2021	6/6/2021	False
7	Acme Singapore	6/6/2021	6/6/2021	False
8	Acme Korea	6/6/2021	6/6/2021	False
9	Sample Account for Entitlements	29/3/2021	29/3/2021	True

Figure 6.19 – The row-level formula field added as a column

In *Figure 6.19*, if you notice rows 4, 6, and 7 have the same Created Date with Last Modified Date, but the result is False, this is because reporting does not show time, only date.

> **Notes**
>
> You only can add one row-level formula in a report. Not all types of fields can be used for row-level formulas, for example, you can't use Boolean, Email, Multi-select picklist, and Time field types. You also can't use row-level formulas for cross-filters or buckets.

Summary Formula

The summary formula is a function to calculate summaries of numerical fields in a report, this function is only available in a report with at least one grouping.

Let's get hands-on to see how this formula works in a report. We are going to calculate the percentage of the Amount of each Stage in an Opportunity report.

1. Create a new report and select report type = **Opportunities**
2. Remove all default fields and add the following fields in the report: `Opportunity Name` and `Amount`, then add `Stage` on **Group Rows**. You can change the filters as necessary, such as change the Close Date to **Current FY**.
3. Make sure to enable **Update Preview Automatically**, otherwise, click the **Refresh** link to update the report with the latest update.

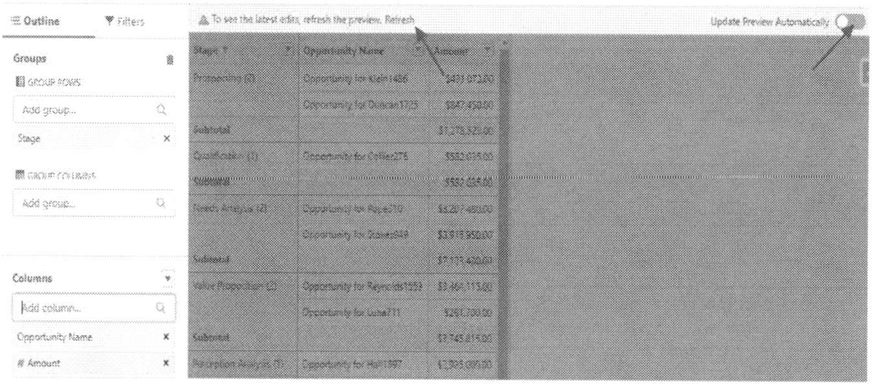

Figure 6.20 – Enable Update Preview or click Refresh link

4. Disable **Row Count** and **Detail Rows** from report footer
5. Click the arrow icon next to **Columns** and select **Add Summary Formula.** If you see in *Figure 6.18*, the Add Summary Formula is disabled because that report does not have grouping.
6. In the **Edit Summary-Level Formula Column** window, enter the following
   - Column Name = `Stage %`
   - Formula Output Type = `Percent`
   - Decimal Points = 2
   - General tab:

```
AMOUNT:SUM/PARENTGROUPVAL
(AMOUNT:SUM, GRAND_SUMMARY)
```

   - Display tab: select **Specific Group**, then Row Group = **Stage**

Figure 6.21 – Create Summary Formula

7. Click the **Validate** button to check, then **Apply** button, and then the **Save & Run** button.

Stage ↑	Sum of Amount	*fx* Stage %
Prospecting	$24,597,662.00	3.05%
Qualification	$53,942,843.00	6.68%
Needs Analysis	$64,842,060.00	8.03%
Value Proposition	$29,715,331.00	3.68%
Id. Decision Makers	$133,017.00	0.02%
Perception Analysis	$38,848,875.00	4.81%
Proposal/Price Quote	$15,889,140.00	1.97%
Negotiation/Review	$17,044,891.00	2.11%
Closed Won	$418,647,239.00	51.86%
Closed Lost	$143,549,999.00	17.78%
Total	$807,211,057.00	

Figure 6.22 – Report with Summary Formula

The report in *Figure 6.22* uses a summary formula to calculate the percentage of the sum Amount of each stage compare to the total.

If your report has **rows** and **columns grouping**, the formula of **PARENTGROUPVAL()** needs to be updated, such as `AMOUNT:SUM/PARENTGROUPVAL(AMOUNT:-SUM, ROW_GRAND_SUMMARY, COLUMN_GRAND_SUMMARY)`

Subscribe to a Report

Subscribing to a report is to schedule the report delivered to your email periodically, instead of you manually logging into Salesforce to see the report update every time you need it.

You can subscribe to reports that you have View access to, you do not need edit access to the report. Each user can subscribe to a maximum of five reports, this count does not include if someone subscribes for you as another Recipient, which we will discuss under **Add Recipients below**.

Permissions

There are 4 permissions related to this function:

1. Subscribe to Reports
2. Subscribe to Reports: Add Recipients
3. Subscribe to Reports: Set Running User
4. Subscribe to Reports: Send to Groups and Roles

You need your Salesforce Admin to enable those permissions as needed, let's go over each of them.

Subscribe to Reports

This is the base permission. Without this permission, you will not see the Subscribe menu under the dropdown next to the Edit button.

Subscribe to Reports: Add Recipients

Enabling this permission will auto-enable **Subscribe to Reports** permission. This permission allows the user to subscribe to other users. Without this permission, the user can subscribe only themself. To add other recipients to the subscription, make sure the report is saved in a shared folder as these visibility permissions will still apply.

Subscribe to Reports: Set Running User

Enabling this permission will auto-enable **Subscribe to Reports** permission too. This permission allows the user to select which user to run the report for on an email subscription, otherwise, the report will run as the user who subscribes to the report. Setting the running to another user is useful when the data is not visible to all users.

Subscribe to Reports: Send to Groups and Roles

Enabling this permission will auto-enable **Subscribe to Reports** permission and **Subscribe to Reports: Add Recipients**. This is similar to Subscribe to Reports: Add Recipients, additionally, the users will be able to select **Group** and **Roles** too as the recipients, otherwise, we need to mention each user name as the recipients.

Report Subscription components

When you configure a report with subscriptions, there are a few items to configure:

Frequency

How often do you want to get the report sent to you? You have options of **Daily**, **Weekly**, **Monthly**. Here you also can define the time, days, and week. The setting here depends on if you select daily, weekly, or monthly.

Attachment

By default, you will see the report result in the email body, however, Salesforce also offers you to get the report result as Excel or CSV attachment on the email. If you choose to get the report as an attachment, you will be able to select to get the attachment as a Formatted Report or Details Only, this is similar to Export data from the report. Additionally, you also need to have **Export Reports** permission to perform this.

> **Notes**
>
> There is a limit of up to 15,000 rows, 30 columns, and 3 MB file size, otherwise, the extra data will not be sent.

Recipients

If you do not have the **Subscribe to Reports: Add Recipients** permission, you will not see the Recipients option, which means the report will only be delivered to you as per the schedule defined.

Run Report As

If you do not have the **Subscribe to Reports: Set Running User** permission, you will not see the option Run Report As, which means the report will be run as you.

Conditions

This is to configure if you **only** want to receive the report email if the report meets certain conditions, such as record count, the sum of amount, etc. You can define multiple conditions. If you do not define this, recipients will always receive the email as per the schedule set.

Hands-on Exercise

We have discussed all the permissions and items that need to be configured to set up a report subscription. Now, let us do a quick hands-on exercise to subscribe to a report. In this exercise, let's use our last report created in the previous subchapter Summary Formula.

1. Open **Summary Formula** created earlier
2. Click the arrow next to the Edit button, and select **Subscribe**, if you do not see this, reach out to your Salesforce admin for the permissions.

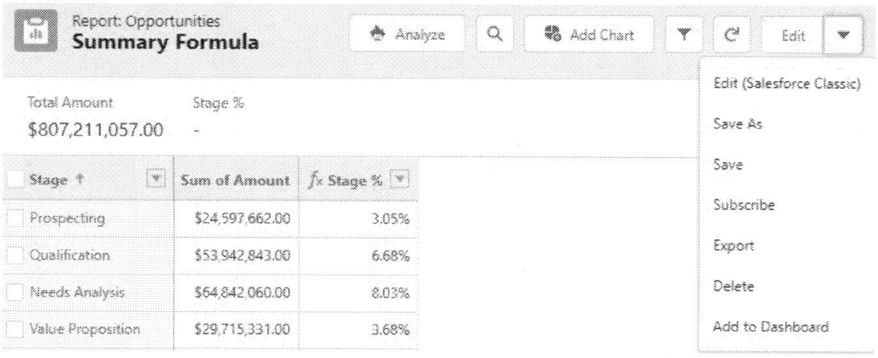

Figure 6.23 – Subscribe report menu

3. You will see the **Edit Subscription** window, follow the screenshot as per *Figure 6.24*, you can change the option as per your user names. You need to have all permissions mentioned above, otherwise, you may see fewer options to be configured. For this exercise, I'll leave out the Conditions setting, so the recipients will always receive the email as per the frequency scheduled.

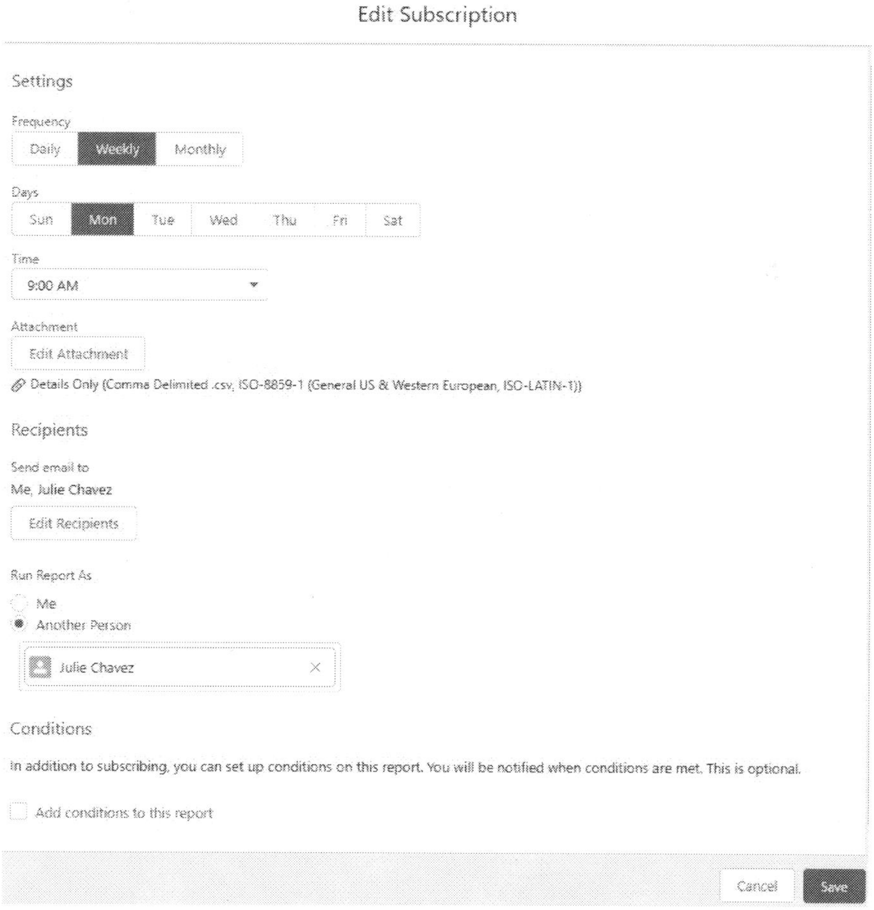

Figure 6.24 – Subscribe a Report

4. Click the **Save** button.

In this subchapter, we learned how to subscribe to a report, where you need additional permissions granted to you. You can configure it to receive the result as an attachment, who will be the recipients, who will run the report for the subscription and adding conditions for when to receive the email.

> **Notes**
>
> To subscribe a user, group, or role to a report, the folder containing the report must be accessible by the user, group, or role.
>
> Lightning Experience report subscriptions don't support Historical tracking reports and Joined reports.
>
> You can subscribe to reports with conditional highlighting, but conditional highlighting doesn't appear in the subscription email.

Add to Dashboard

We will discuss Dashboards in depth in *Chapter 7* but for now, we will learn a function to add a report into the dashboard, whether it is to an existing dashboard or as a new dashboard.

To perform this, simply open any report and click Add to Dashboard. Let's do a quick hands-on exercise to add the report to a new dashboard

1. Open the Summary Formula report created earlier and click **Add to Dashboard** from the arrow next to the Edit button

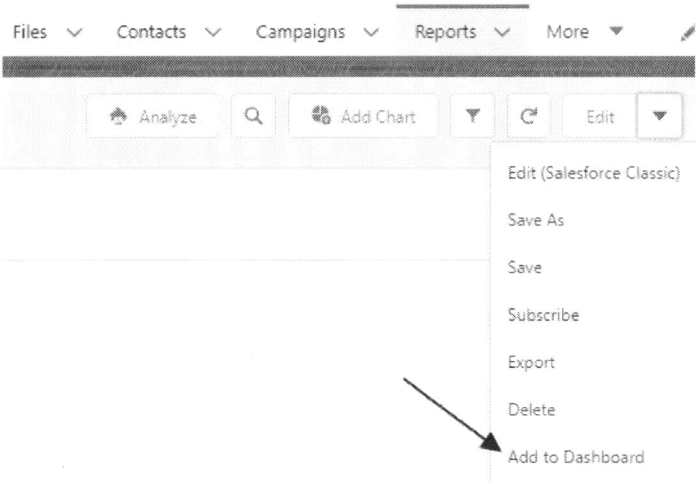

Figure 6.25 – Menu Add to Dashboard

2. Select **Add to new dashboard**, and enter the Name = `Opportunity Stage`, and keep the folder as Private Dashboards.

3. Click the **Add** button to continue
4. You will be presented with Add Component window, keep everything as it is, then clicks the **Add** button
5. Drag the component width to cover the whole dashboard area
6. Click the **Done** button, click the **Save** button to continue

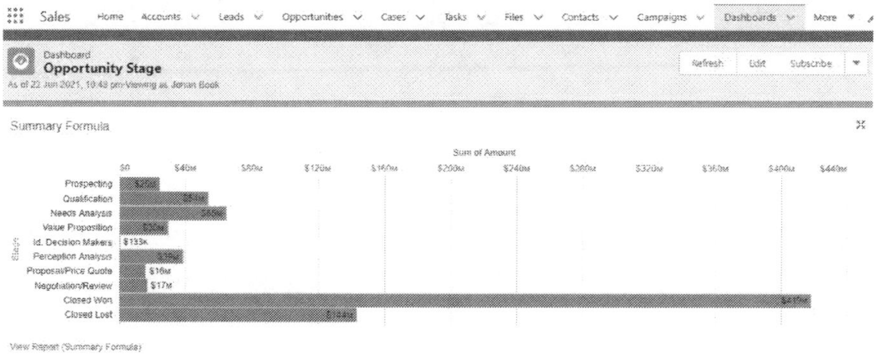

Figure 6.26 – Adding a report to a new dashboard

Export Report

Salesforce offers the ability to export report result into Comma Delimited format .csv, and Excel format .xls or .xlsx, but you must have **Export Report** permission.

There are 2 views you can select:

1. Formatted Report – as per report style in Salesforce
2. Details Only – raw data of the report

For Formatted Report, you only have the option to export into Excel file .xlsx, this makes sense as the .csv file does not support format/styling. While for detail only, you can select any formats mentioned, and you can select the encoding, this is important if your report contains non-English characters, such as Arabic, Chinese, Japanese, Korea, etc.

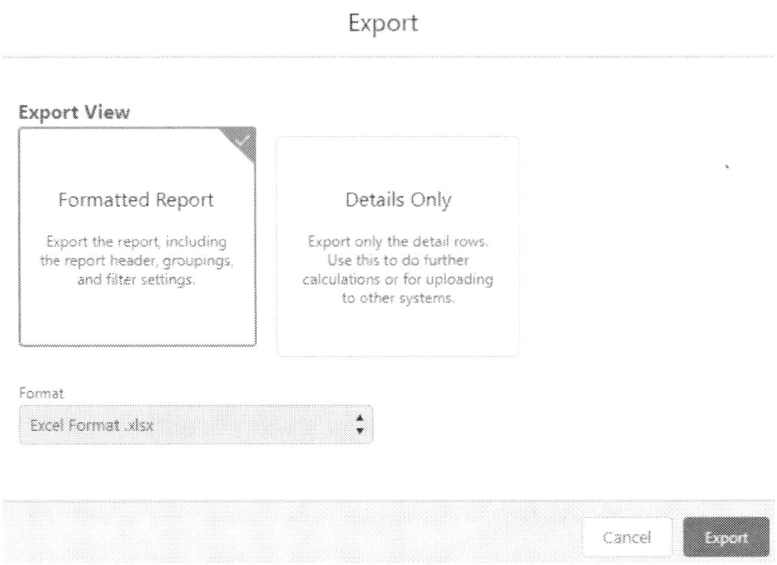

Figure 6.27 – Export View option when Export a Report

Summary

In this chapter, we learned a lot of features that can be used when building a report, but that does not mean we need to use all of the features available in one report. Here are a few best practices related to this chapter:

- Always add parentheses in the report logic in the report filter, this will make sure the system executes the logic in order. Make use of the comma in the report filter of a field if it contains multiple values
- Make use of the cross filter to show data with or without a child object
- Drill Down is useful when you need to analyze a report
- Report Parameter can be used to change filter values on the fly, and the complete URL can be added as a bookmark in the web browser
- Unique Count will show you how many unique values of a column
- Make use of a Bucket Column to categorized values into a new column
- The row-level formula can be used to compare or calculate fields in a report
- The summary formula is good to use if you need to calculate value across a report
- Make use of Report Subscriptions to deliver reports to your and your team's Inbox when most useful
- We can add a report into a dashboard directly from a report
- You can export the report and selecting the right view, if you just need the raw data, select Details Only.

- Make use of the relative date in the report filter when needed, like TODAY, YESTERDAY, NEXT WEEK, LAST 30 DAYS, and so on

In the next chapter, we will learn about Salesforce Dashboards, including tips and best practices in building and sharing dashboards with your team members.

CHAPTER 7:

BUILDING DASHBOARD

Dashboard visualizes the data stored in a system, within a glance, we can see the trend and issues with our business, such as pipeline, closed-won deals, active cases, etc. Dashboard in Salesforce is built on reports as the data source. Every component in the dashboard must have a report set as the data source, but you can use the same report for multiple components in a dashboard.

In *Chapter 5, Reporting on the Cloud,* we learned the foundation of Salesforce reporting, and the good thing is, the dashboard foundation is very similar to the report foundation, such as folder, favorite, tab, and permissions. If you are not familiar with those items, please check back to *Chapter 5, Reporting on the Cloud.*

In this chapter, we will learn features of the Salesforce dashboard, here are the topics:

- Dashboard Folder
- Dashboard Permission
- Concept of Dashboard
- Dashboard Component
- Dashboard Filter
- Dashboard Theme & Palette
- Dynamic Dashboard
- Subscribe to Dashboard

Dashboard Folder

In the report, you can create ad-hoc reports, which means, you create an ad-hoc report and get the result without the need to save it, however, in the dashboard, when we create a dashboard, ideally, we should save it for future use, or share it with our teams, it does not make sense to create a dashboard for one-time use only, so the dashboard should store into a dashboard folder.

The folder concept in the dashboard folder is very similar to the report:

- Use folder to set user access: manage, edit and view
- The same concept of subfolder

The difference with the report folder is, there is no **Public folder** for the dashboard, whether to save it in the Private folder or to a "team" folder for sharing.

Because the dashboard folder is very similar to the report folder, we will not discuss this again here.

Dashboard Permission

Same with report permissions, each user needs to have permissions to create dashboards and dashboard folders. The permissions name for the dashboard is also very similar to the permission name for the report, simply change from **report** to **dashboard**, such as **Create and Customize Reports** to **Create and Customize Dashboards**, the same permission also applies for the folder, manage public, view all, and subscribe. But there are a few permissions that are only applied for the dashboard:

- Change Dashboard Colors
- Manage Dynamic Dashboards
- View My Team's Dashboards

We will discuss the above permissions later in this chapter. If you are unable to follow exercises later in this chapter, such as missing buttons or menus, that's mean you do not have the permission, so reach out to your Salesforce admin to enable it for you, via your profile or through a permission set.

Same as the folder, we will not repeat to discuss permission again here.

Concept of Dashboard in Salesforce

Not Real-time

Different from the report, opening a report will always show the latest data in the system, however, opening a dashboard will show data as of when the last user refreshed it. If you need to see the latest data in the dashboard, you need to manually click the **Refresh** button, and this is allowed only once in a minute.

There is a way to schedule the refresh, we will cover that later in this chapter.

View as

This is also another difference with reporting, when you open a report, the data show is based on your visibility, but when you open a dashboard, it shows the data based on someone's visibility, the dashboard builder will set this when building the dashboard.

Again, there is a way to set the dashboard view as yourself, even further, you can change the dashboard **view as** someone from your team member, so you can see how is their data, we will also cover this later in this chapter.

Data source

Every component in the dashboard must have a data source, and the data source here is a **report**. You can make use of the same report for multiple dashboard components. Report type and report setup will determine things that can be configured in the dashboard component, such as a tabular report only can be displayed as a Table, not as a Chart.

The report used as a data source must be accessible by the "view as" user, whether stored in a team folder or public folder.

Drill-down

As mentioned earlier, every dashboard component has a report used as the data source. The report used as the data source is displayed as a link at the bottom left of the component, if you need to see the data, click the report link. However, the report opens with data as per running user visibility, **which is you**, not as the "view as" user set in the dashboard. If you don't have access to the report, you will get an error message, the data visibility is per your Salesforce profile.

If the component is displayed as a chart, click a bar from the chart will open the report used as the data source, and further, it will auto **add a filter** to the report, based on the grouping clicked in the dashboard. From the report, click the report filter will show the additional **Linked Filters**.

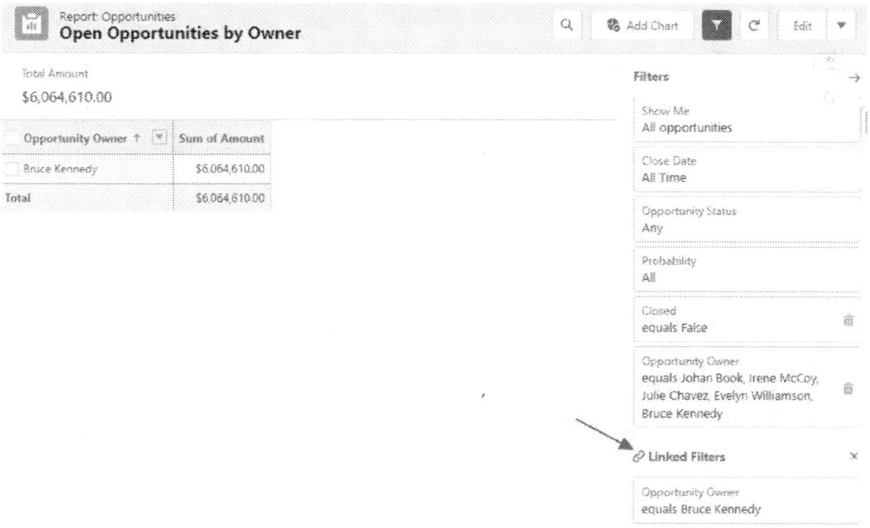

Figure 7.1 – Linked Filters in Report

Dashboard Component

A dashboard in Salesforce usually consists of multiple components, you can add up to 20 components in a dashboard. Each component needs to have a report used as the data source, and the same report can be used in multiple components in a dashboard.

The components in a dashboard can be mixed with different types of charts or tables. Each component does not interact with the other components but will interact with dashboard filters. You can have different sizes of components, also a different theme for each component.

Component Setting

If the report used as the data source contains a chart, you can use it directly for the dashboard component, otherwise, you need to select the chart/table. Each chart has its setting, such as X-Axis, Y-Axis, Decimal Places, Sort By, etc., but general items are applicable for all charts, such as Title, Subtitle, Footer, Theme.

To edit a component, you must edit the dashboard first, then click the pencil icon at the upper right corner of the component. In the dashboard edit mode, you can move the components around, also resizing the component.

Gauge Component

There are 11 types of charts/tables that you can choose for a component, from the horizontal bar chart, vertical bar chart, and so on until the lightning table. We will not discuss each component in this book, however, there is one interesting component, this component is good to show the current value versus target, which is the **gauge chart**.

In the Winter 22 release, which is around Oct 2021, Salesforce announces dynamic gauge chart mode, this gives you the ability to set the target value in a record, not in the component itself. Without dynamic mode, you must enter the zero, low, medium, and target values manually in the component. You just need to set the low and medium percentages of the target in the component.

Best Practice

By using dynamic gauge charts, updating the target value in an object is much faster and less human error. Create a custom object to store the target value, then use inline editing in the list view to update all targets easily, ideally create additional fields to store dashboard name, component name, description, and owners, with this, you can easily identify each record is used for which dashboard and component.

To use a dynamic gauge chart, your Salesforce admin needs to enable it from the setup menu by selecting **Enable Dashboard Dynamic Gauge Charts (Lightning Experience only)**.

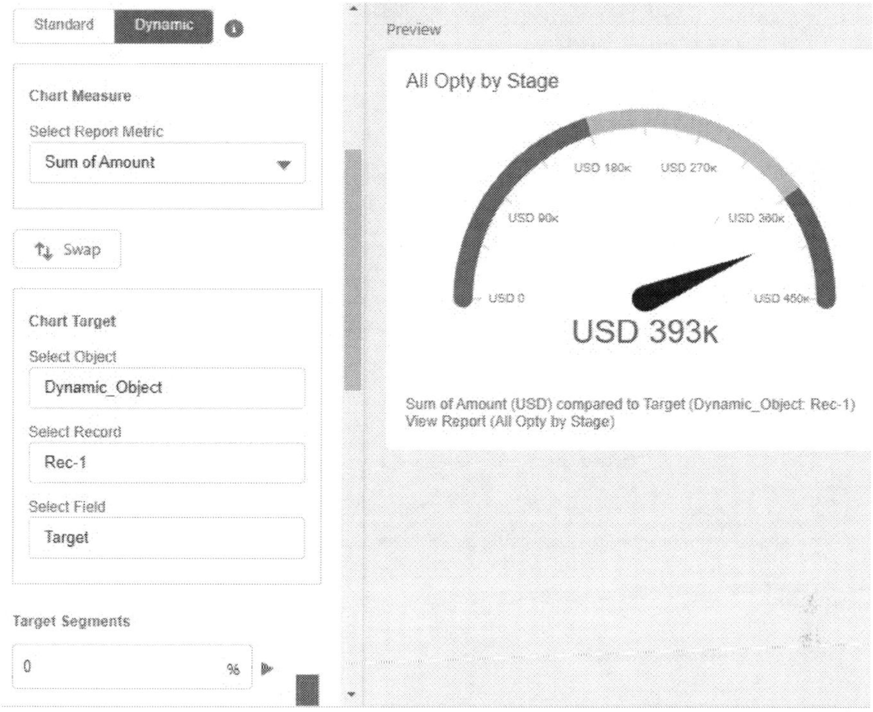

Figure 7.2 – Dynamic Gauge Chart

Dashboard Filter

Another powerful feature available in the dashboard is the dashboard filter, you can add up to 3 filters in a dashboard. All components in the dashboard will be filtered based on selected values.

With this, imagine that you have a global sales dashboard and if the executives would like to see how the APAC, EMEA, and AMER regions perform, instead of creating multiple dashboards, simply add a Region filter. Also, it is much easier to maintain a dashboard rather than 4 similar dashboards (for Global, APAC, EMEA, and AMER), however, users will be able to select each region, so no data confidentiality here.

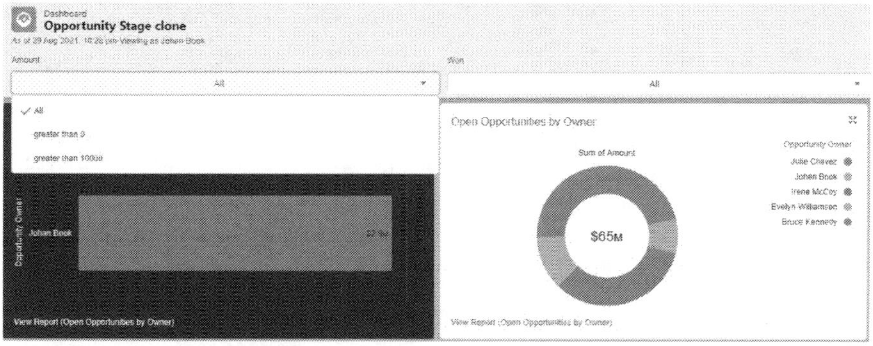

Figure 7.3 – Dashboard with Filters

Dashboard by default will remember the last filters that you selected, so the next time you open the dashboard, it will be auto filters with those values.

Using Parameter

Similar to the report, you can use URL parameter too to filter the dashboard, and the good news is, the way it works is very similar to the report filter. Simply add **fv0** for the **1**st filter after the original URL, **fv1** for the 2nd, and **fv2** for the 3rd filter.

If your dashboard URL is *https://bookcom3-dev-ed.lightning.force.com/lightning/r/Dashboard/01Z5g000000cuEzEAI/view* and you would like to pre-set the 3rd filter with a value, simply add **?fv2=text** at the end of the URL, for example, *https://bookcom3-dev-ed.lightning.force.com/lightning/r/Dashboard/01Z5g000000cuEzEAI/view?fv2=Qualification*

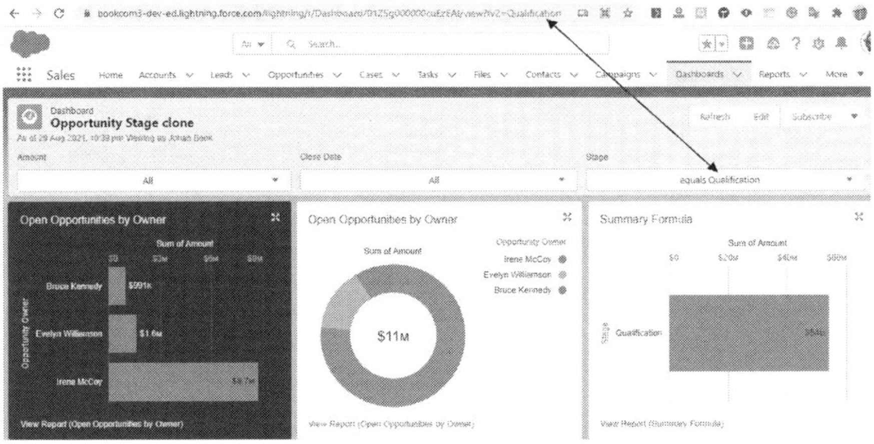

Figure 7.4 – A filter added to dashboard URL

With this, you can share the URL to users that need the dashboard to be filtered with a set of values, the user can bookmark the URL in their web browser.

Dashboard Theme and Palette

To have the ability to change the dashboard theme and palette, you must have **Change Dashboard Colors** permission. If you have this permission, when editing the dashboard, click the gear icon, then you will see options for Dashboard Theme, which is Light and Dark, and also 14 color options for the Dashboard Palette.

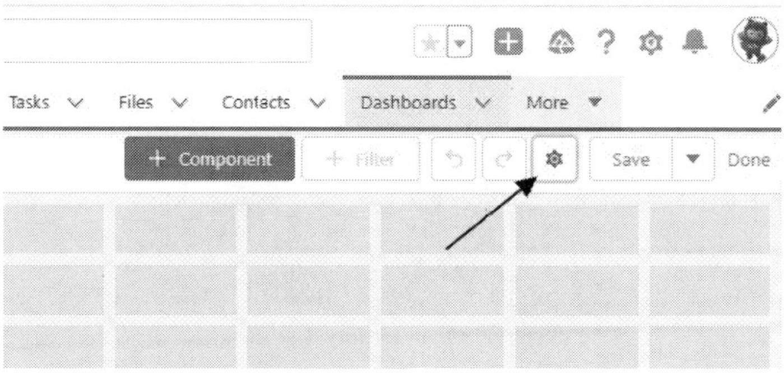

Figure 7.5 – Edit Dashboard Properties

When you create a new dashboard, by default, the theme is Light, and Palette is Aurora. As a dashboard builder, you can change the color and palette the beautify the dashboard.

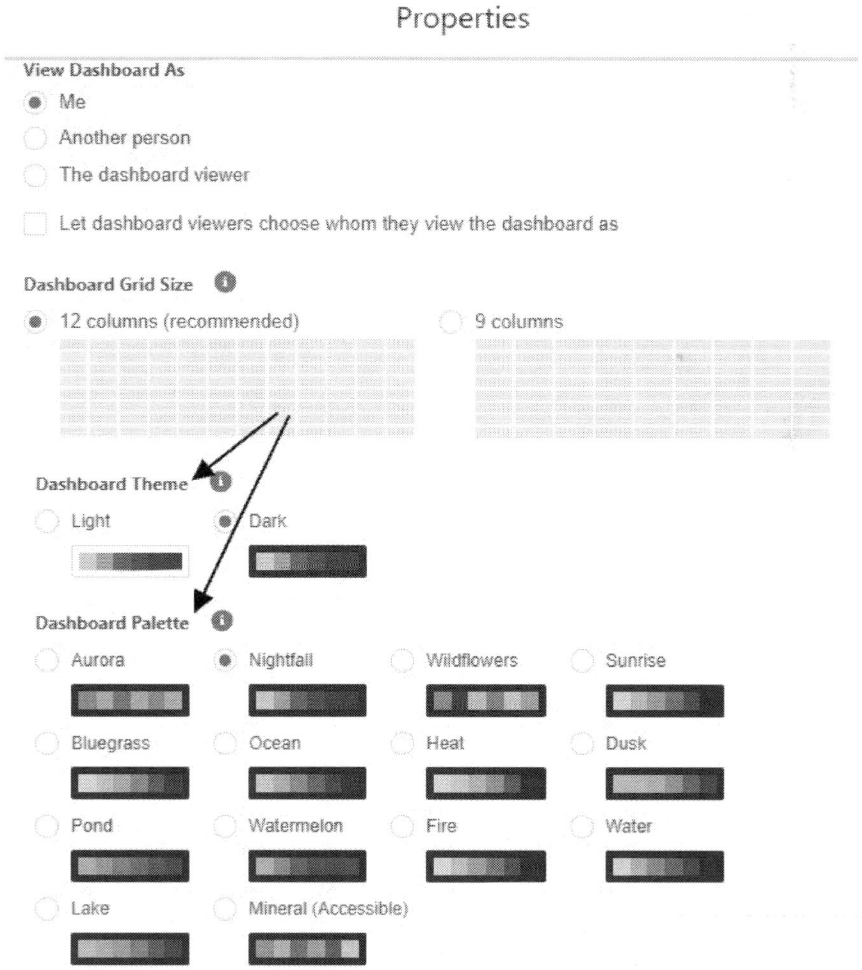

Figure 7.6 – Dashboard Theme and Palette

Component Theme

In addition to the Dashboard Theme, there is also Component Theme. When you change the Dashboard Theme to Dark, the Component Theme for all components will be automatically changed to Dark too, however, you can update the theme for each component different from the dashboard theme.

To update the component theme, when from dashboard edit mode, click edit component (pencil icon), then scroll down to Component Theme.

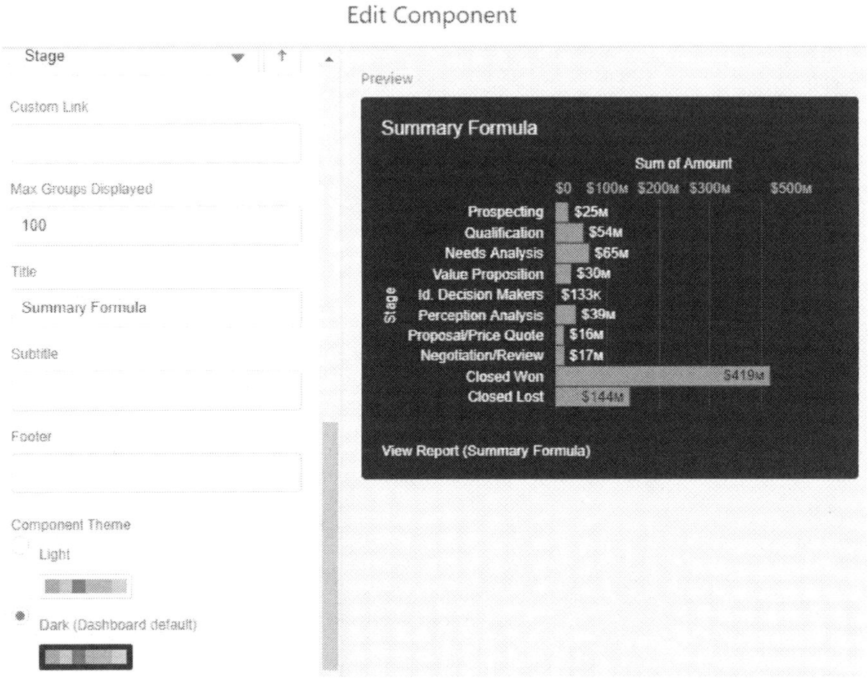

Figure 7.7 – Component Theme

Dynamic Dashboard

As mentioned in the Concept of Dashboard subchapter, data in the dashboard is shown based on the data of the "view as" user. However, Salesforce also offers the capability to show the data as the login user or as someone in your team, a user under your role hierarchy.

> **Notes**
>
> Only a maximum of 5 dynamic dashboards can be configured in Enterprise Edition and 10 in Unlimited Edition.

To create or edit a dynamic dashboard, you need to have **Manage Dynamic Dashboards** permission. If you have this permission, when creating or editing the dashboard, you will have the option to select "The dashboard viewer" under "View Dashboard As", this option will let the login users see data based on their visibility.

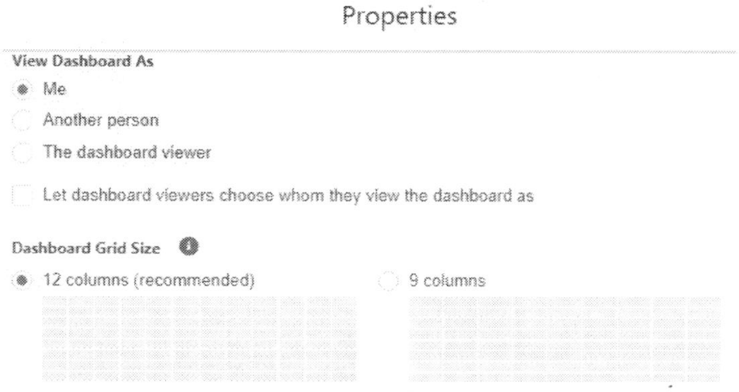

Figure 7.8 – Building Dynamic Dashboard

Furthermore, there is an option of **Let dashboard viewers choose whom they view the dashboard as**, this allowed the dashboard viewer to select someone else in the team member, this only if the login user has **View My Team's Dashboards** permission.

For a dynamic dashboard with "Let dashboard viewers choose whom they view the dashboard as" enabled and the dashboard viewer has "View My Team's Dashboards" permission, the viewer can select a user under his/her role hierarchy.

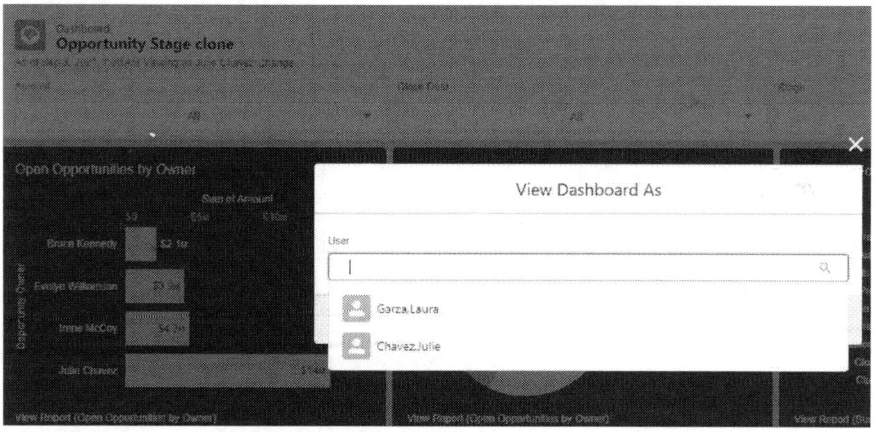

Figure 7.9 – Select a user for View Dashboard As in Dynamic Dashboard

Notes

To build a dynamic dashboard, there are two permissions related here, the dashboard creator needs to have **Manage Dynamic Dashboards** permission, while the dashboard viewer needs to have **View My Team's Dashboards** permission for the ability to select a user as "view as" from beneath the role hierarchy.

Subscribe to Dashboard

In *Chapter 6, Advanced Reporting Features,* we learned that we could subscribe to a report the get the report to deliver to our email. A similar feature is also available in the dashboard too, when you subscribe to a dashboard, the system will auto-refresh the dashboard too, so you or other users who receive the email will get the updated dashboard. The schedule can be daily, weekly, or monthly.

There are 3 permissions related to this function on the dashboard:

1. Subscribe to Dashboards
2. Subscribe to Dashboards: Add Recipients
3. Subscribe to Dashboards: Send to Groups and Roles

You need your admin to enable those permissions as needed, let us see each of them.

Subscribe to Dashboards

- Enabling this permission will auto-enable **Run Reports** permission. Without this permission, you will not see Subscribe button after opening a dashboard. If you subscribe to a dashboard with filters, the dashboard delivered in the email will not have any filters applied.
- There is an option when subscribing to a dashboard **Receive new results by email when dashboard is refreshed**, if you do not select this checkbox, no email will be delivered, so subscribe to the dashboard will simply refresh the dashboard only at the selected time. This answer on how we can refresh a dashboard automatically.

> **Notes**
>
> There is a maximum of 5 dashboards a user can subscribe to. You cannot subscribe to a dynamic dashboard, the Subscribe button is simply not visible in the dynamic dashboard.

Subscribe to Dashboards: Add Recipients

Enabling this permission will auto-enable **Subscribe to Dashboards** permission. This permission allows the user to subscribe to other users, without this permission, the user only can subscribe to him/herself. To add other recipients to the subscription, make sure the dashboard is saved in a shared folder.

Subscribe to Dashboards: Send to Groups and Roles

Enabling this permission will auto-enable **Subscribe to Dashboards** permission and **Subscribe to Dashboards: Add Recipients**. This is similar to Subscribe to Dashboards: Add Recipients permission, additionally, the user will be able to select Group and Roles too as the recipients, otherwise, the user needs to mention each user name as recipients.

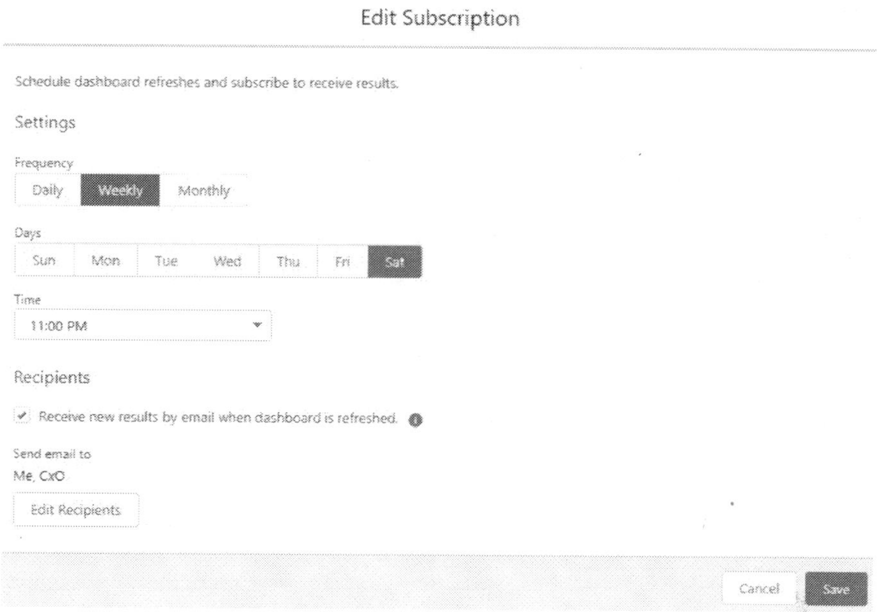

Figure 7.10 – Subscribe a Dashboard

To unsubscribe from a dashboard, simply click **Subscribe** button on the dashboard, then click **Unsubscribe** button at the lower left of the Edit Subscription window.

Creating a Dashboard

We have discussed all dashboard features in Salesforce, but it will not be completed if we do not have a hands-on exercise to create a dashboard. In this hands-on, we will create a dashboard to show Open Opportunities by Stage and by Opportunity Owner, we will also add filters with Close Date and Amount.

1. Create a report folder called **Pipeline Report** and a dashboard folder called **Pipeline Dashboard**
2. Share both folders to Public Group = **All Internal Users**

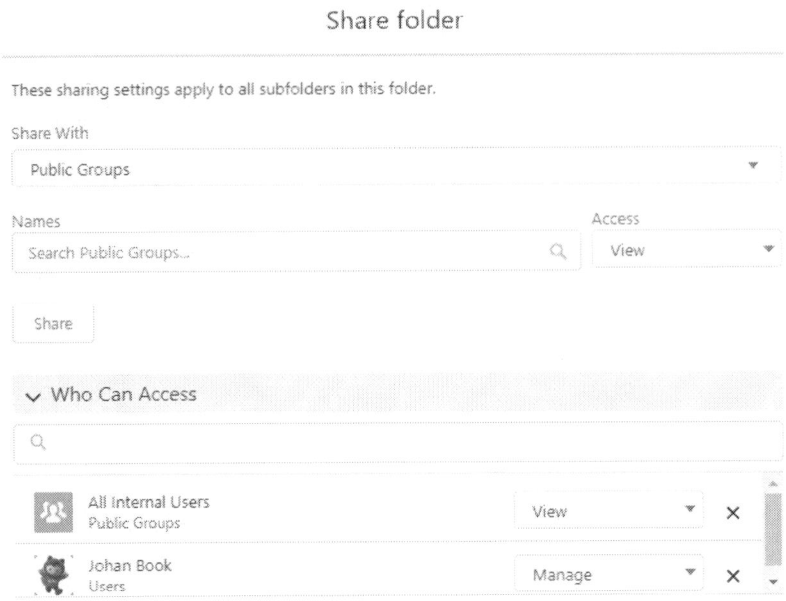

Figure 7.11 – Sharing a folder

3. Create a report with the following setup:
   - Report Type = Opportunities
   - Remove all default columns
   - Add following columns: Opportunity Name, Stage, Close Date, Opportunity Owner, and Amount
   - Move Stage and Opportunity Owner to Group Rows
   - Change report filter to Close Date = All Time, Opportunity Status = Open
   - Turn off all options at the bottom: Row Counts, Detail Rows, Subtotals, Grand Total
   - Save the report as Pipeline under the Pipeline Report folder
   - Run the report and you will see the report group by Stage and Opportunity Name

Report: Opportunities
Pipeline

Stage ↑	Opportunity Owner ↑	Sum of Amount
Prospecting	Bruce Kennedy	$224,800.00
	Catherine Brown	$1,666,850.00
	Chris Riley	$3,082,260.00
	Dennis Howard	$1,420,100.00
	Doroth Gardner	$89,230.00
	Eric Gutierrez	$858,070.00
	Eric Sanchez	$1,312,950.00
	Irene Kelley	$2,102,240.00
	Irene McCoy	$4,381,760.00
	John Williams	$206,640.00
	Julie Chavez	$2,217,555.00
	Kelly Frazier	$431,073.00
	Laura Garza	$136,464.00
	Laura Palmer	$5,198,280.00
	Nicolas Weaver	$1,269,390.00
Qualification	Bruce Kennedy	$991,350.00
	Catherine Brown	$1,821,769.00

Figure 7.12 – A pipeline report

4. Click the **Dashboard** tab, then click the **New Dashboard** button, if you do not see the button, reach out to your Salesforce admin to grant you permission

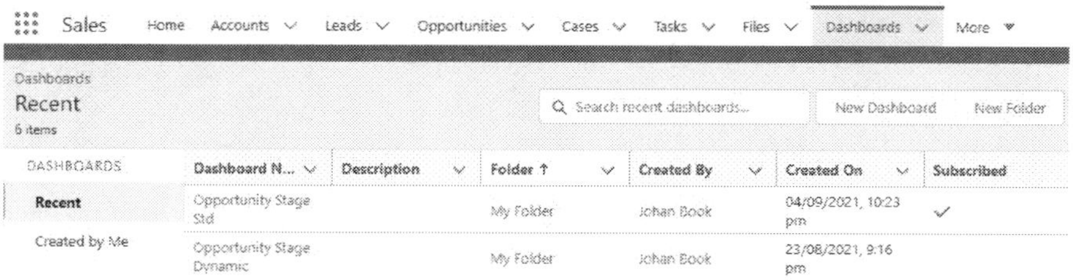

Figure 7.13 – Dashboard tab

5. For dashboard name, enter "All Pipeline" and stored it in the "Pipeline Dashboard" folder created earlier.
6. Now you should see a blank canvas with 12 boxes horizontally, click the **+ Component** button

7. Select Pipeline report created earlier, then click **Select** button
8. Let us use the default Horizontal Bar Chart, delete Opportunity Owner from Y-Axis
9. Click **Add** button

Figure 7.14 – Add Component to Dashboard

10. Click **+ Component** button again and select the same report
11. Select Opportunity Owner from Y-Axis and delete Stage
12. Click **Add** button
13. The 2nd component will be added below 1st component, drag the 2nd component at the right of 1st component
14. Let us make the 2nd component wider by dragging the right border of the component
15. Rename the 1st component title by clicking the pencil icon on 1st component, scroll down to **Title** and change it to **Pipeline by Stage**, click the **Update** button
16. Do the same for 2nd component by changing the title to **Pipeline by Owner**
17. Click the Save button, then Done.
18. Now you should have something similar to *Figure 7.15 - A draft dashboard*

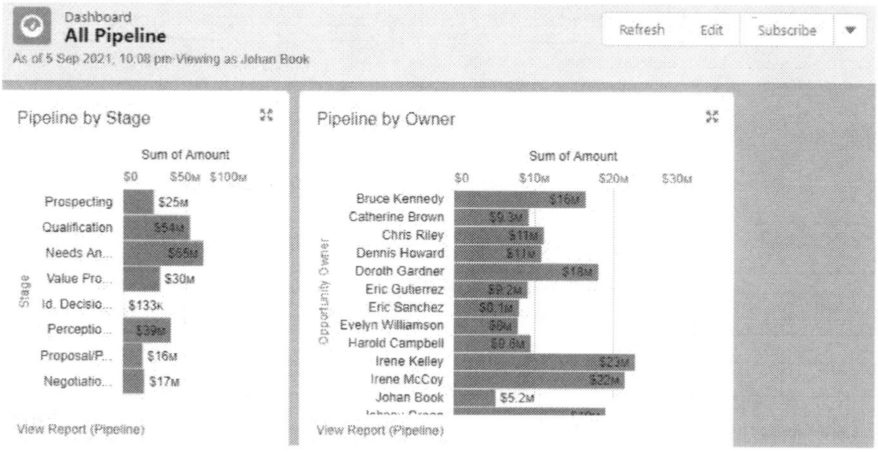

Figure 7.15 – A draft dashboard

Let us continue to add 2 filters: Amount and Close Date

19. Click Edit button
20. Click + **Filter** button
21. Type **Amount**, then click **Add Filter Value** button
    - 1st value: Operator "less than", Value = 1000, Display Text = < 1000
    - 2nd value: Operator "between", Starting Value = 1000, Ending Value = 10000, Display Text = 1000 – 10000
    - 3rd value: Operator "greater than", Value = 10000, Display Text = > 10000
22. Click **Add** button
23. Click + **Filter** button again
24. Type **Close Date**, then click **Add Filter Value** button
    - 1st value: Operator "equals", Date Type = Relative, Value = Next 30 Days, Display Text = Next 30 Days
    - 2nd value: Operator "equals", Date Type = Relative, Value = This Fiscal Quarter, Display Text = This Fiscal Quarter
25. Click **Add** button
26. Click the Save button, then Done.
27. Now you should see 2 filters added to the dashboard and feel free to try by selecting each filter with different values

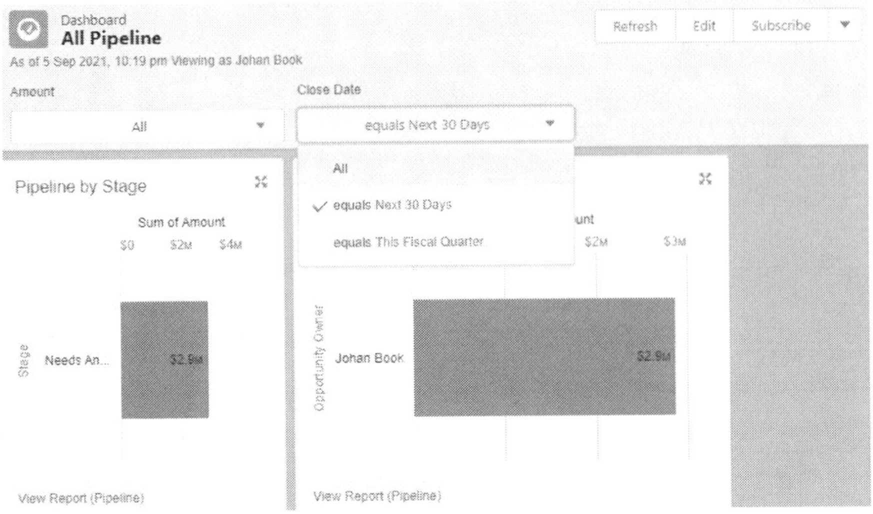

Figure 7.16 – A draft dashboard

28. Finally, let us change the dashboard theme to Dark
29. Click the Edit button then click the gear icon
30. Scroll down to the bottom and select Dark from Dashboard Theme
31. Click Save button, Save again then Done
32. Now our dashboard theme changes to Dark in a few clicks

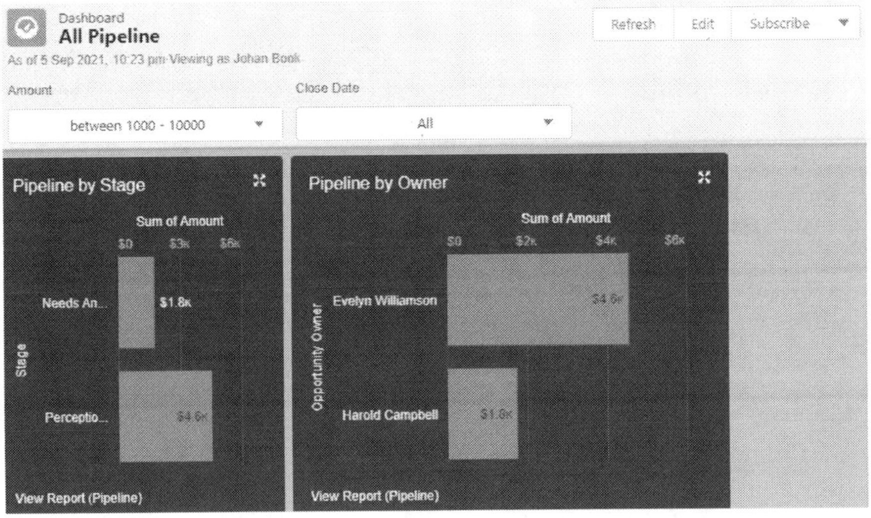

Figure 7.17 – Dashboard in Dark theme

Summary

In this chapter, we learned a lot of features in the Salesforce dashboard, and we end with creating a dashboard from scratch, start by creating a report and dashboard folder, share the folders to all internal users, create open opportunities report, create a dashboard, add components, add filters, and change the dashboard theme.

Here are a few best practices related to the dashboard:

- Make use of the Dashboard folder and subfolder to organize dashboards properly
- Not all users should have all permissions related to the dashboard, such as only the admin or operational team allow to create folders, all other users should request this from the admin team
- Stored all reports used as the data source for the dashboard in a report folder that accessible by all dashboard viewers, as they may drill down the dashboard
- Selectively configure dynamic dashboard as just needed, because there is a limit of the dynamic dashboard that can be created
- You can use the same report for the different components if the data is similar, but for different visualization
- Make use of dashboard filters, rather than create many similar dashboards, for example, a pipeline dashboard for APAC and another dashboard for EMEA
- Make use of the subscribe dashboard feature to refresh dashboards and to get the dashboard delivered to your and your team's email.

CHAPTER 8:

SALESFORCE MOBILE APP

When your company purchases Salesforce licenses, it comes with the mobile app too, which means you can simply download the mobile app from App Store (for iPhone) or Google Play Store (for Android). By right, your admin does not need to configure anything for you to use the mobile app, however, for optimal experience, your admin should enable the lightning app for the mobile experience.

In this chapter, we will learn Salesforce mobile app, here are the topics:

- Installation and login
- User interface
- Offline
- Customization
- Working in mobile app
- Installation and Login

As a smartphone user, you should know how to install an app easily, and there is no difference to install Salesforce mobile app. Just search **Salesforce** in the App Store or Google Play Store and follow the instruction. Once completed, you should see a new app with the Salesforce logo as the app icon. The first time you open the app, it will ask you for the login credential.

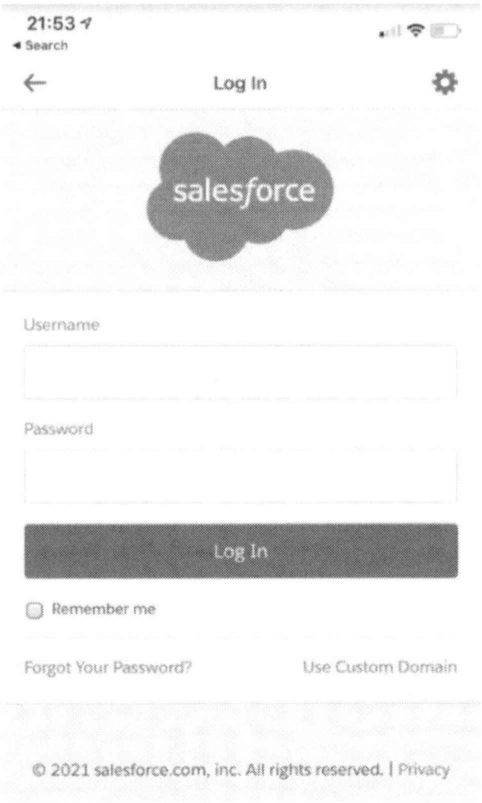

Figure 8.1 – Salesforce mobile app login screen

Enter the same username and password as you normally enter to log in to Salesforce from a web browser, if your company uses SSO for authentication, tap "Use Custom Domain" and follow the step.

The app may ask you to verify your identity when logging in for the first time from a new device, then you may get an SMS or email to verify, depends on your Salesforce setup, enter the verification code and tap **Verify** button. Next, another prompt that asks you to allow access to the Salesforce app, tap **Allow** button, and this should let you enter the app.

User Interface

The first time you log in to Salesforce, you will see **Chatter**, unless your Salesforce admin has configured a lightning app for you or all Salesforce users. If you see Chatter, you will notice there are 5 icons at the bottom of the app: Chatter, Today, Dashboard, Tasks, and Menu.

Lightning app

To make sure you are using the correct lightning app in the mobile app, tap **Menu** > **App Launcher** > select Lightning app that you normally use in the web browser. In *Figure 8.2*, I will tap **Sales** as that is the app that I use in the web browser, but your app name may be different. If you are unsure what is the app name that you use in the web browser, check the label after the 9-dots icon, see *Figure 8.3*, which is "Sales" for mine, yours can be different.

Mobile Only app is the default app, and it is not synced with the Lightning app, so don't select this app, unless your company has a specific arrangement.

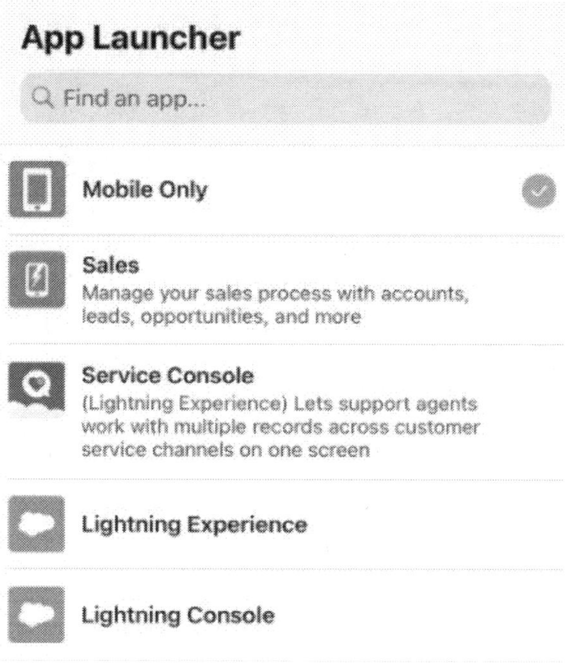

Figure 8.2 – App Launcher

Once you select the correct Lightning app, you will see the familiar menu as you see in the web browser. *Figure 8.3* will show the menu under the Sales app that I select earlier, you will see a different set of menus for your app, which is fine.

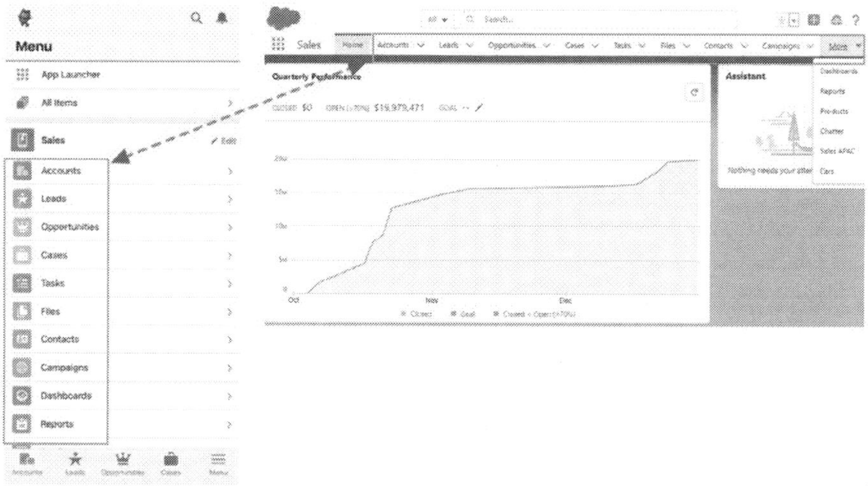

Figure 8.3 – Items in Menu align with tabs in the browser

If you realize, the order of the menu in the mobile app is the same as the tab that you arrange in the web browser, simply because they are the same Lightning app.

You can re-order the menu from the mobile app by tap the **Edit** link, then drag and drop the menu to move the menu as your preference, the order changed here will reflect in the web browser tab too. Tap any menu here will open the tab.

> **Tips**
>
> The icons at the bottom of the mobile app are the same as the first four tabs after the Home tab in the Lightning app. Therefore, always put the most used tabs at the left part in the navigation bar, as they will appear as icons at the bottom of the mobile app. The 1st icon will be the landing page when opening the app.

In the web browser, you can access all menu items from the 9-dots icon, in the mobile app, tap the **Menu** icon at the bottom right > **All Items**, see the left screenshot in *Figure 8.3*, you should see all items that you have access to, you also can search the item by typing the name in the search box.

> **Notes**
>
> The Home page and Utility Bar are not available in the mobile app, but there is something new introduced in Winter '22 release (October 2021) called **Mobile Home**, your admin need to enable this feature.

Favorite

In *Chapter 1, Customizing My User Interface*, we mentioned that list of Favorites is accessible from anywhere, including from the mobile app.

To access favorite from the mobile app:

1. Tap your avatar at the top left corner of the screen
2. Tap **Favorites** menu
3. All your favorite items should be here, and you also can search by typing the name

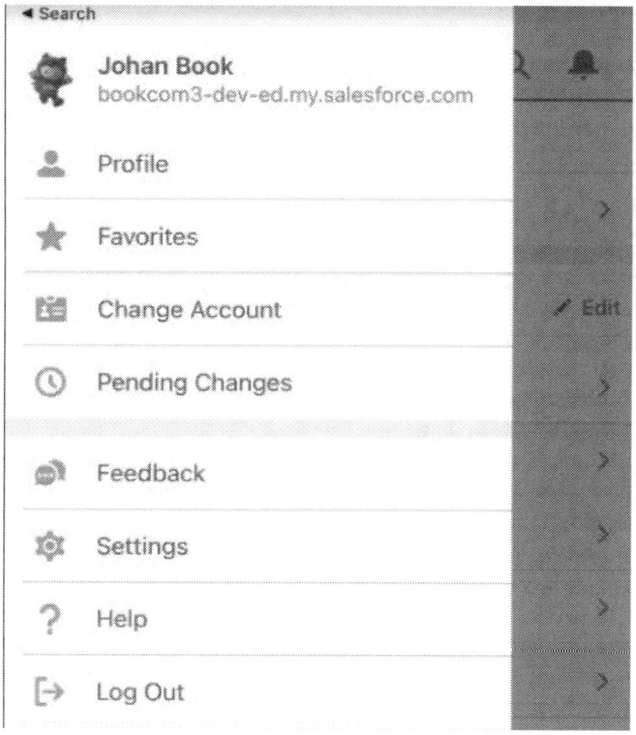

Figure 8.4 – Accessing Favorite in mobile app

To add a record into favorite:

1. Open the record that you want to add as a favorite, such as an opportunity
2. Tap favorite (star icon) at the top
3. Once added, the star icon will be filled

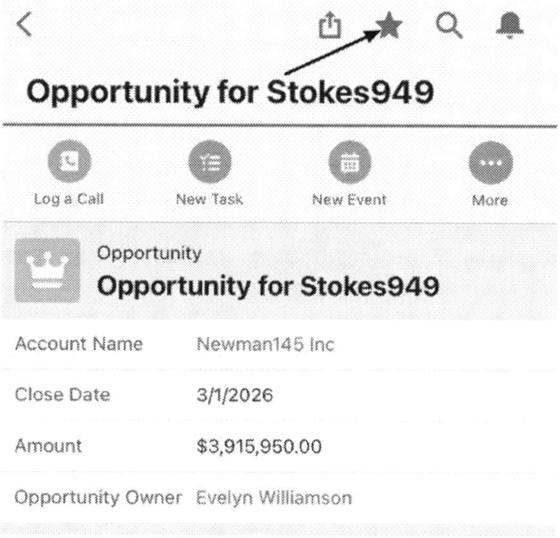

Figure 8.5 – Adding a record as Favorite

Tips

Only add records and items that you often used or will be used or check in the future, having too many items added to your favorite list is not helpful and disorganized, so always clean up and remove obsolete items from your favorite.

List View

All list view that you have in the web browser is available in the mobile app too. To access the list view, open the object, such as Opportunity, this will show Recent List View and Recent Opportunities that you open. To see all list views, tap the **All Lists** menu, this will show all List View that you have access to, you also can search the list view by typing the name.

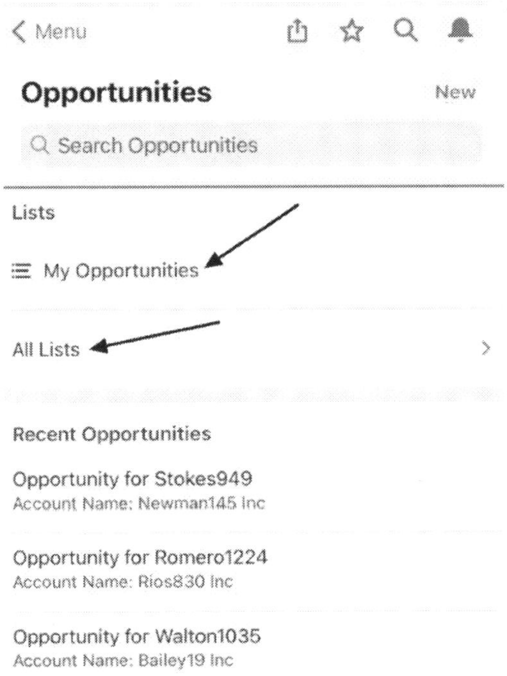

Figure 8.6 – Accessing recent List View and All List Views

Tips

You can create your personal list view by log in to Salesforce from the web browser, check out *Chapter 2, The Power of List View*. The personal list view created will be available in the mobile app too.

Search

Similar to the web browser, we can search from the mobile app as well. You can search using the same keyword, such as Account Name, Account Number, and so on.

There are 2 ways to search in the mobile app:

1. Click the magnifying glass icon at the top right of the screen (next to the favorite icon), this will search all objects that you used often
2. Open a menu, such as Account, then search in the textbox provided, this will search records from Account only

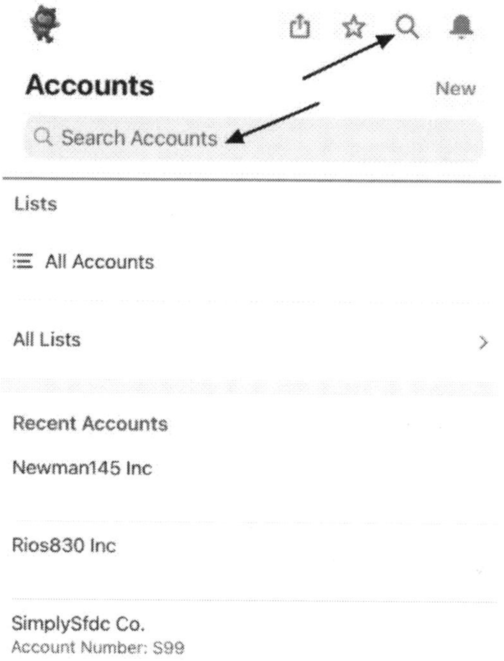

Figure 8.7 – Search in mobile app

> **Tips**
>
> Searching by record name is always works, however, Salesforce does not search all fields, so make sure you enter the correct name, such as for Opportunity Name. The search result in mobile is the same as in web browser, for more information on searching, check out *Chapter 4, Searching the Data.*

Notification

Next to the Search (magnifying glass) icon is the Notification icon, this is the same Notification icon as you see in the web browser.

When someone mentioned you in Chatter, you will see the notification here, to take this further, if you enable notification on your mobile phone for the Salesforce app, you will see the message pop up in your mobile phone. Depends on your Chatter notification setting, you may receive an email notification too, check out *Chapter 3, Collaborating with Chatter* to configure your Chatter notification.

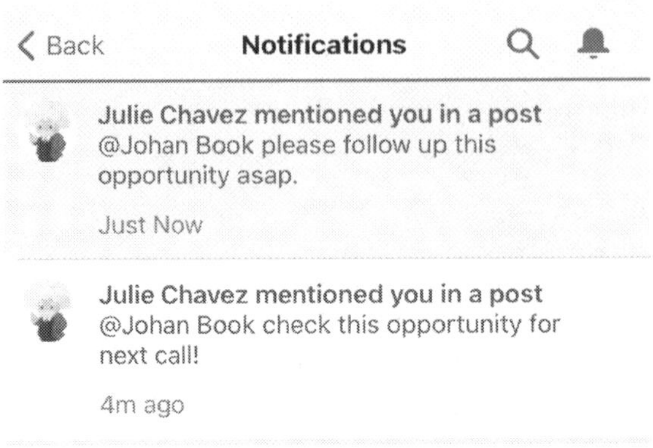

Figure 8.8 – Notification in mobile app

Sharing

The icon at the left of the Favorite (star) icon is Sharing icon, this feature is only available in the mobile app, not in the web browser. The purpose of sharing here is to share a record with your team member, such as sharing an Opportunity link to your team member via **any type of communication tool installed in your mobile phone**, from Email, SMS, WhatsApp, Hangouts, etc.

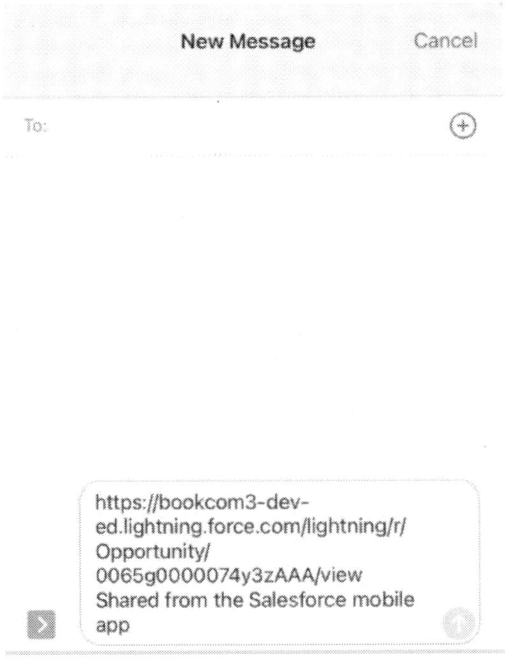

Figure 8.9 – Sharing a record link using SMS

Offline

By default, Salesforce mobile app supports offline access, which means, you still can use Salesforce mobile app even there is no internet connection on your mobile, but only up to 30 records were recently accessed in the last 5 objects. Recently accessed means, records that you accessed last from mobile app and web browser.

You also can configure what objects that you want to access offline, by selecting up to 7 objects to be accessible offline. Tap your **avatar** > **Settings** > **Offline Preferences**

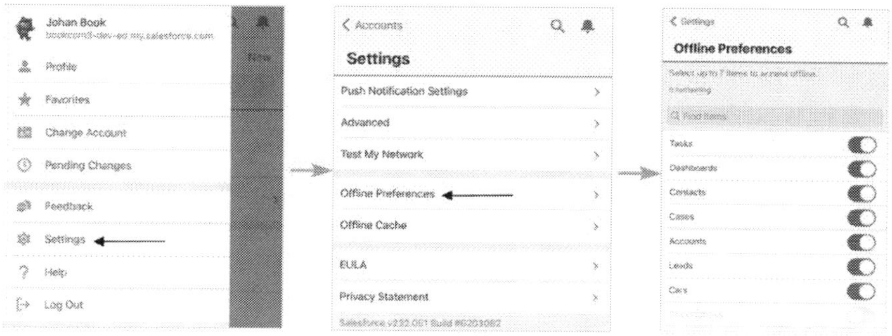

Figure 8.10 – Offline Preferences

Offline Cache

If you know that you will have no internet connection soon, you can start offline caching, follow *Figure 8.10*, tap **Offline Cache**, below Offline Preferences, then tap the **Start Caching** button, it will also show you when is your last cached.

What can you do when offline?

You can read the record that you accessed recently, but not searching. You also can edit those records accessed recently, once saved the record, you will see a green icon on the record, which identifies the record has been updated offline.

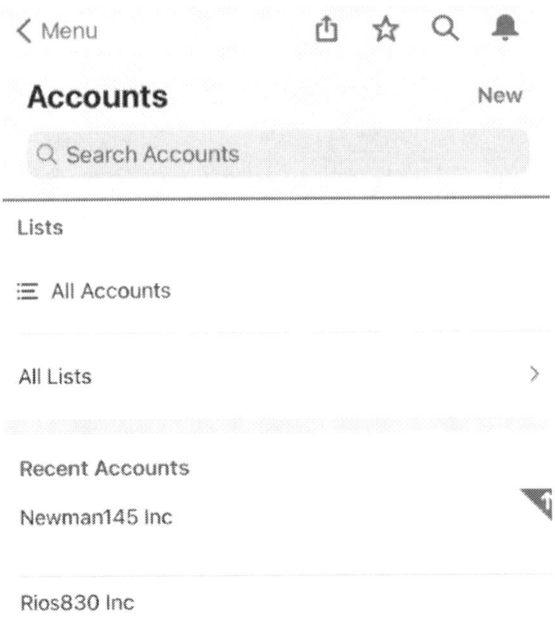

Figure 8.11 – A record that has been updated offline

To see all records have been updated offline, tap your avatar > **Pending Changes**, here you will see all records have been updated offline from your mobile app.

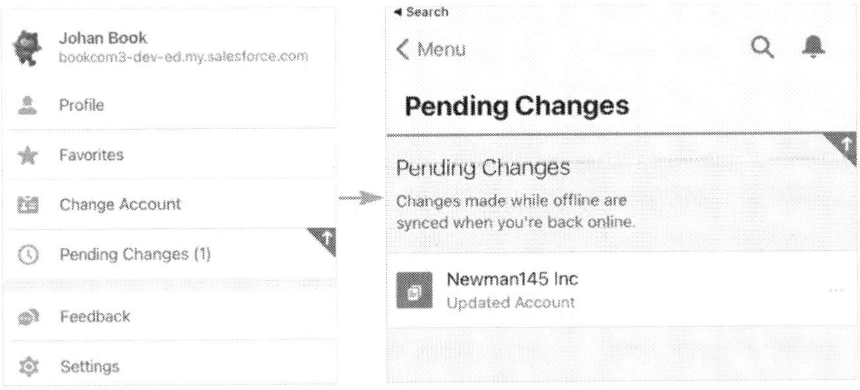

Figure 8.12 – Monitor pending changes

Once your mobile phone is connected to the internet, opening the Salesforce app will auto-sync the changes to Salesforce. If there is a conflict, such as a record has been updated by someone else, you will see an orange icon for you to solve that manually.

Additionally, you also can create new records when offline, such as a new Lead or Contact. Same as edit, you will see a green arrow for new records created, they will appear in the Pending Changes too. Once sync to Salesforce, items in Pending Changes will be removed.

Customization

What can we customize in Salesforce mobile app? As discussed earlier in this chapter, we can move the menu order, which also updates the tabs order in the web browser, the first 4 menus will appear as icons at the bottom of the mobile app.

Another customization on the Salesforce mobile app is **branding**, this only can be done by your Salesforce admin. It is good to match the Salesforce mobile app with your company's color and logo. Items that can be customized for branding:

- Brand Color
- Loading Page Color
- Loading Page Logo

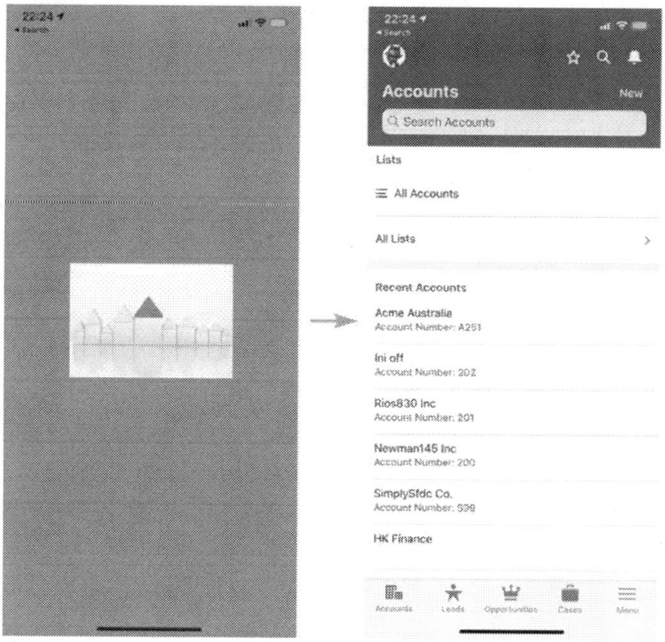

Figure 8.13 – Mobile app with new branding

Figure 8.13 shows a customize page color and logo when loading the app, this ideally should match your company colors and logo.

Working in Mobile app

How to use Salesforce mobile app? It is similar to all other mobile apps, you just need to open the app and play around, by searching, open records, create records, however, you also can call, email, log a call directly from your Salesforce mobile app.

Let us have a quick look at working with the mobile app, for example, I am on the road and would like to call John Lee, he is COO of SimplySfdc Co.

Here are the steps:

1. Open the Salesforce mobile app, enter the login credential if needed
2. You will be landed to the 1st object in the menu order, such as Account or Contact or Opportunity
3. For example, if you set Account as the 1st tab, you will see
   - Recent Account list views opened
   - Recent Account records opened
   - Search Accounts textbox
   - New icon (to create a new account), only if you have permission
   - Share, Favorite, Search, and Notification icon
   - Four object icons at bottom and Menu at bottom right

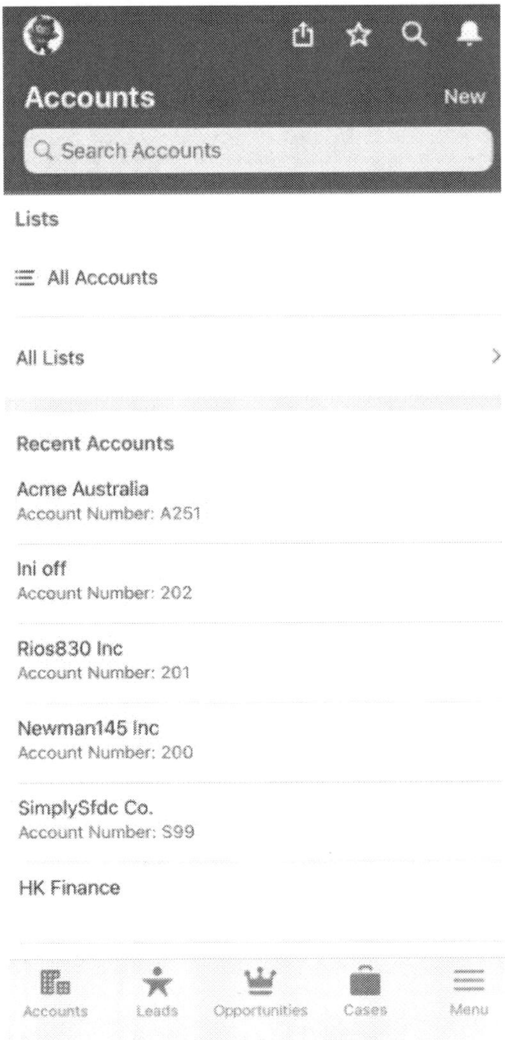

Figure 8.14 – Mobile app landing page

4. As I already know the contact that I would like to call, type "John Lee" from the search icon on the upper right corner, however, in scenario if I only remember the company name, I will search the Account name and looks for contact
5. Tap the search icon and type John Lee, if you open that contact recently, you will see it directly, and tap it to open the contact, otherwise, hit the Search

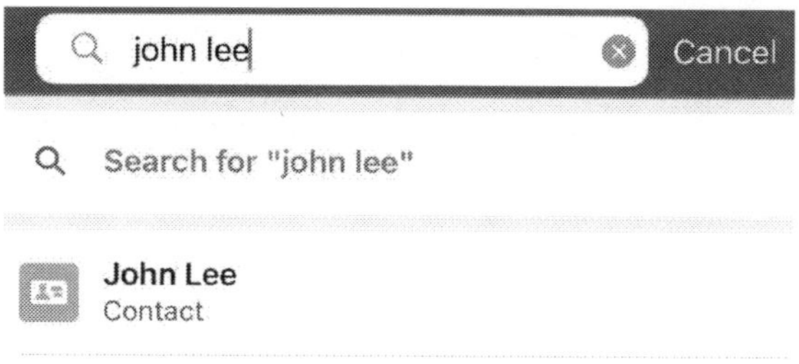

Figure 8.15 – Recently access records

6. Tap the contact from the search result to open it

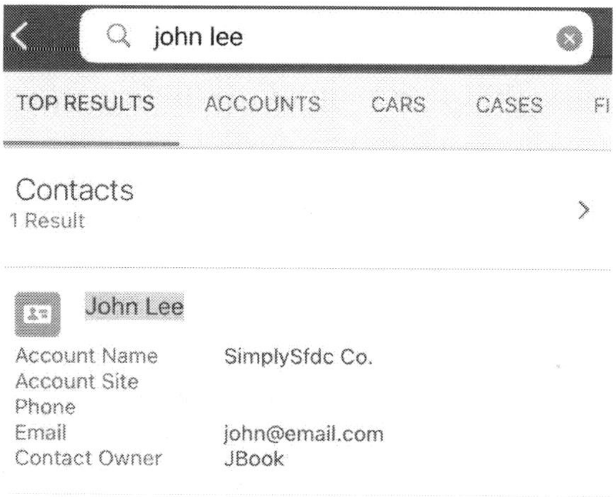

Figure 8.16 – Search result

7. Depends on the actions configured by your Salesforce admin, by default, you will see the **Call** icon, if you don't see it, tap the **More** icon, from here you can directly call the contact if the phone number is entered.

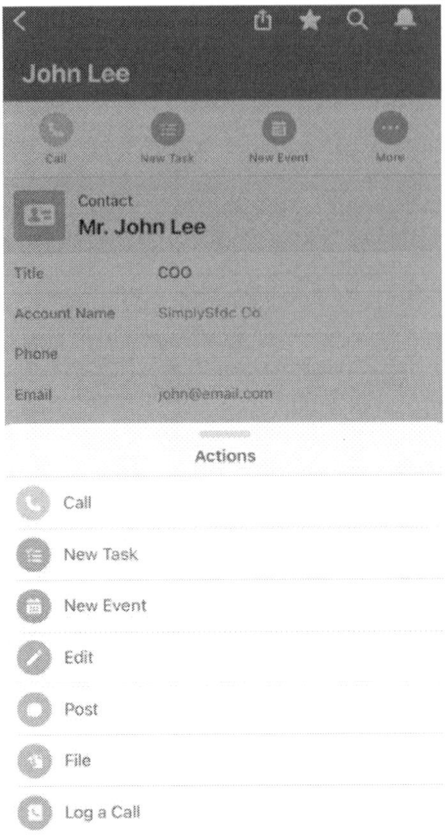

Figure 8.17 – Take Actions

8. Once your call ends, since the call is still fresh in your mind, you can directly Log a Call from here, see *Figure 8.17*, this will create a closed task and logged to that contact. Additionally, you can edit, create a new event or new task, or edit the contact to update or add some information.
9. All the updates and data entered are stored in Salesforce directly or will sync to Salesforce if you are offline.

Summary

Finally, we reach the last chapter of this book, however, there is an appendix chapter *Setting up My Salesforce Setting*, so make sure you check out the appendix too.

In this chapter, we learned about the Salesforce mobile app, which is included as part of the licenses of Salesforce and is available for both iPhone and Android phones.

Here are a few best practices related to mobile app:

- Make use of the app as no additional license or cost is needed
- By default, your admin does not need to configure anything for you to use the mobile app

- For users that are always on the road, accessing Salesforce from a mobile phone would be a great benefit, so do share with your colleagues to have this app on their mobile phone
- On average, you can use the mobile app to do 70-80% of your Salesforce work, things that cannot do from the mobile app, such as create a report or dashboard. However, basic needs such as read, edit, create records are available, also the ability to run reports and dashboards.
- Salesforce mobile app supports offline mode, only for record access recently, you can do offline cache if you expect will have no access to the internet. You can also edit and create records when offline, this will sync to Salesforce once your mobile has access to the internet.
- Reach out to your Salesforce admin to customize the mobile app branding to follow your organization's branding.

APPENDIX:

SETTING UP MY SALESFORCE

Firstly, you should be able to login to Salesforcc.com, otherwise, please consult with your organization's Salesforce admin or consultant to ensure you have access. In this appendix, you will learn about the items related to setting up your Salesforce profile after you have logged in. We will cover:

- Setting up My Avatar
- Setting up My Personal Information and Advanced User Detail
- Setup of My Email Setting and Encoding

Setting up My Avatar

The first time you log in to Salesforce, you will notice a grey avatar in the upper right corner of the Lightning page. Salesforce calls this character **Astro.** It is recommended to personalize your Salesforce by changing this avatar to your own photo, your profile picture can be a JPG, PNG, or GIF, with a maximum size of 16 MB.

Update My Avatar

1. Click your **avatar** on the upper right corner of your Salesforce Lightning page (1)
2. Click **your name** (2)

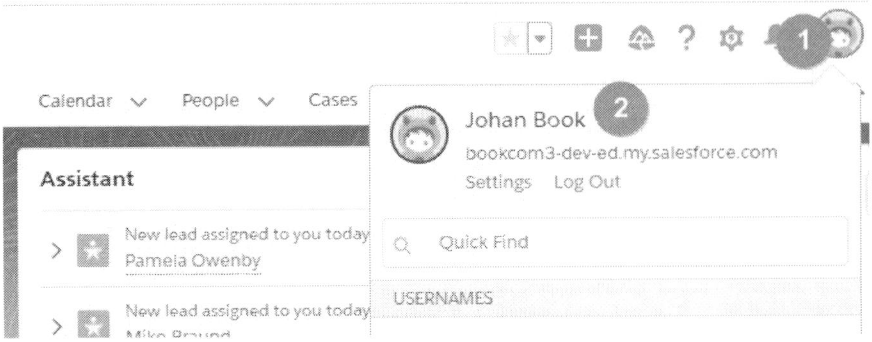

Figure A.1 – Update your avatar

3. Click the **camera icon** (3)
4. Select **Update Photo** (4)

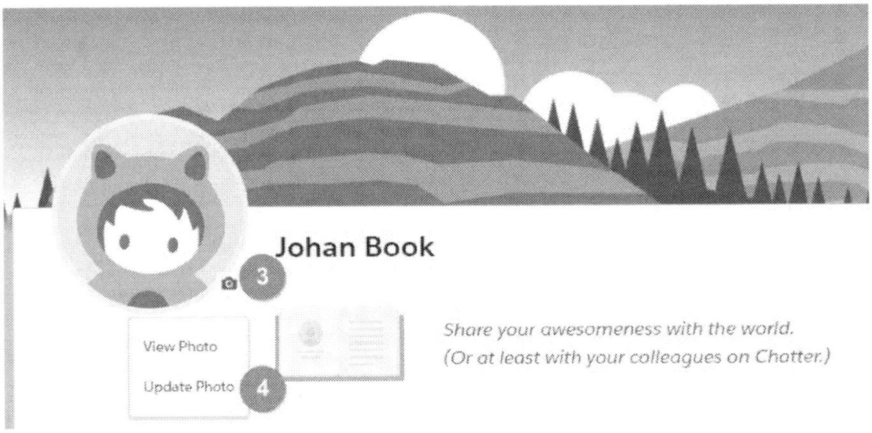

Figure A.2 – Update your photo

5. Click **Upload Image** (5)
6. Locate your photo, and adjust the thumbnail size by dragging the slider (6), if necessary
7. Click **Save** (7)

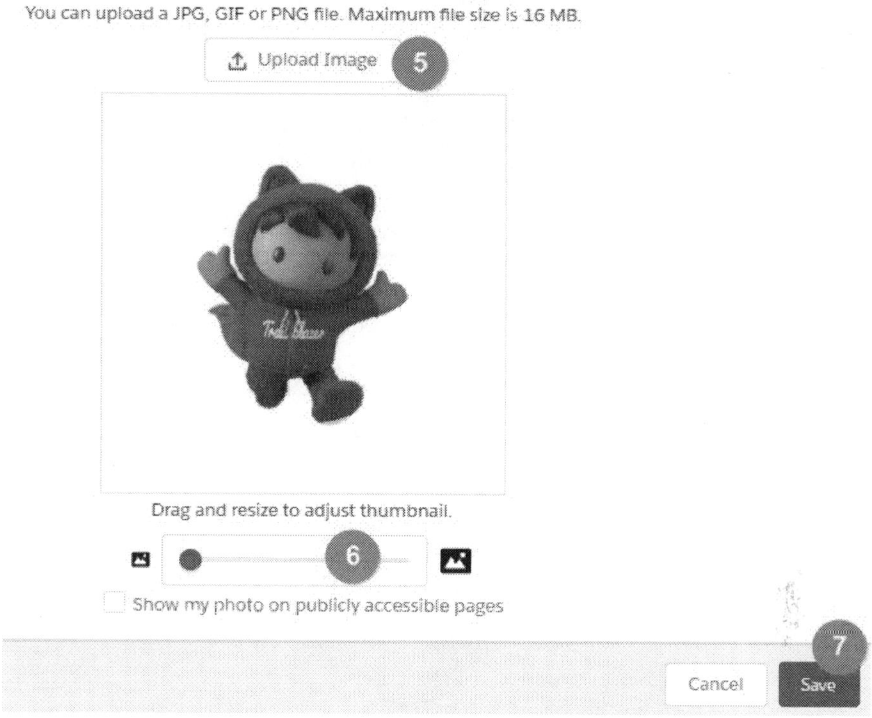

Figure A.3 – Upload and saving photo as the avatar

Why do I need to update my Avatar?

When you are working in a large organization across countries and time zone, in addition to your name, your co-workers will recognize you better when you update your avatar with your own photo.

This photo will appear in many places, including:

- The Chatter feed
- Record ownership
- User lookup fields
- Dashboards

As in *Figure A.4* below, your photo will appear on the dashboard if **Show Chatter Photo** is enabled

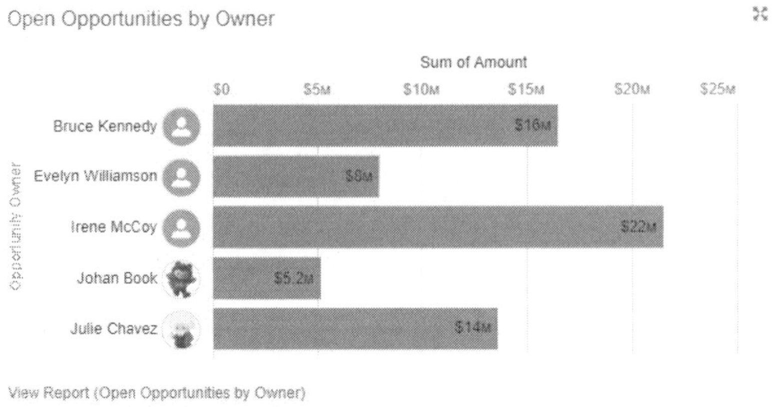

Figure A.4 – Your photo on a dashboard

Your photo will also appear on the record page in the ownership field as well as on user lookups fields, an example in *Figure A-5*, where we have it as a lookup for *Customer Success Manager*.

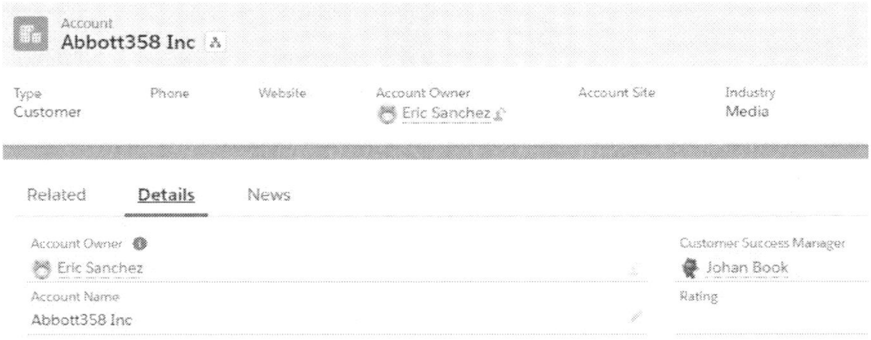

Figure A.5 – Your photo on the Account page

Setting My Personal Information and User Detail

It is very important to set up our Salesforce account with the right information. With the correct setup, you will ensure accurate data is shown correctly and more efficiently for you and others using the same system.

It is easy to set up your personal information so, let's start now.

Set up My Personal Information

1. Click your avatar on the upper right corner of your Lightning page
2. Click **your name**
3. Click the **Edit** button
4. You can update contact fields including your name, phone, mobile, address, title, and department.

Figure A.6 – User page

> **Best Practice**
>
> Make sure your personal information is updated correctly. When your colleague clicks your name on record pages including from Account owner, Opportunity owner, or other user lookup fields, your user information will be presented. So, it is always important to ensure your information is correct.

Set up My User Detail

Under your User Details, you can configure items that are related to how the system will interact with you, such as language, locale, time zone, etc.

1. Click your avatar on the upper right corner of your Lightning page
2. Click **your name**
3. Click the **User Detail** button
4. Click the **Edit** button
5. Locate **Time Zone**, **Locale,** and **Language.** If you see incorrect information selected; you can correct it from here.
6. Click the **Save** button when done.

Why do I need to set up My User Detail?

When your Salesforce admin or consultant creates your Salesforce profile, your user detail may be set up incorrectly. You can fix this by yourself, in addition to name, mobile, phone, title, etc., there are four important items that you should check:

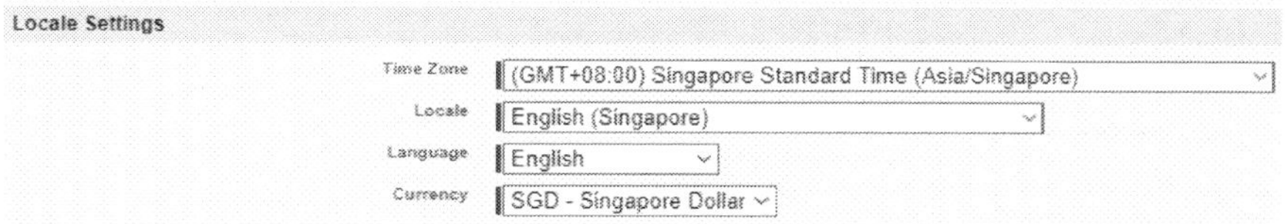

Figure A.7 – Locale Settings

1. Time Zone

Time Zone is important because all data shown in the system is based on your time zone setup in your user detail. This time zone setup impacts many areas of the system, from the page layout, subscriptions, and reports, etc. So, always make sure your time zone is set up correctly.

Sample:

If your time zone is set to Pacific Daylight Time, but you are based in Singapore, when you see an Account created on 28/3/2021, 11:59 pm, this time is Pacific Daylight Time, not Singapore time. However, if you adjust your time zone correctly, it will show as 29/3/2021, 2:59 pm.

In *Figure A.8*, opening an account creation information where my time zone is set to Singapore Time.

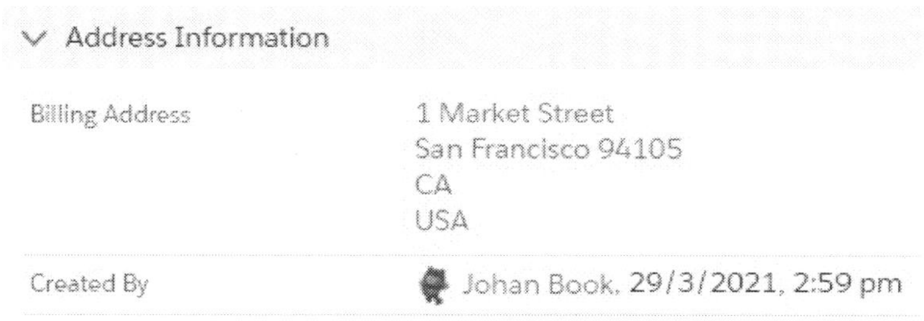

Figure A.8 – Created Date as Singapore Time

Figure A.9 shows the same account view by other users with the time zone set to Pacific Daylight Time.

Figure A.9 – Created Date as Pacific Daylight Time

> **Use Case**
>
> If you are based in Sydney Australia, but your time zone is US Pacific Time, when you run a report and filter to a specific date, such as "2-Dec-2021", the result you get may be wrong or no result as the system recognizes you are as being in the US time zone. Therefore, always make sure your time zone settings are correct.

2. Locale

Locale settings will determine your date-time format, number format, name order, address format, and phone number format, this is also very important. This setting is applied in many places in Salesforce, from the page layout, reports, etc., so, always make sure your locale is set up correctly.

Sample:

If your locale is set up as English (United States), you will see an Opportunity created on 3/29/2021, 2:59 PM, but if you adjust to your locale such as English (Singapore), it will show as 29/3/2021, 2:59 pm.

In *Figure A.10*, opening an account creation information where my locale is set to English (Singapore)

Figure A.10 – Locale set to English (Singapore)

Figure A.11 shows the same account view by other users with locale set to English (United States)

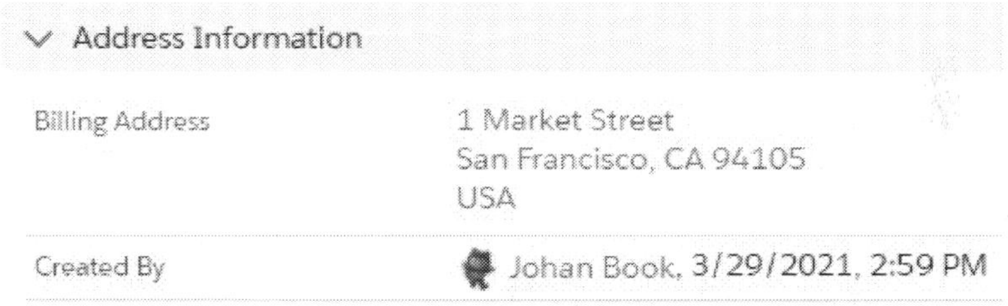

Figure A.11 – Locale set to English (United States)

Use Case

For example, your name is "Bob Smith" and you set your Locale = Chinese, if someone from your team creates a report with filter your name "Bob Smith" as Account Owner, the report will run fine for your colleague, but when you run the report, you see no data because of your locale setting, the system gets your name as "Smith Bob".

3. Language

As you would expect your Salesforce language will display as per your language selected in your user detail settings. Be careful if you try to select other languages, to make sure you can read that language first, otherwise you may find it hard to change back to your original language. If that happens, reach out to your Salesforce admin to have it updated for you.

Sample:

In *Figure A.12*, opening an account creation information when my language is set to English

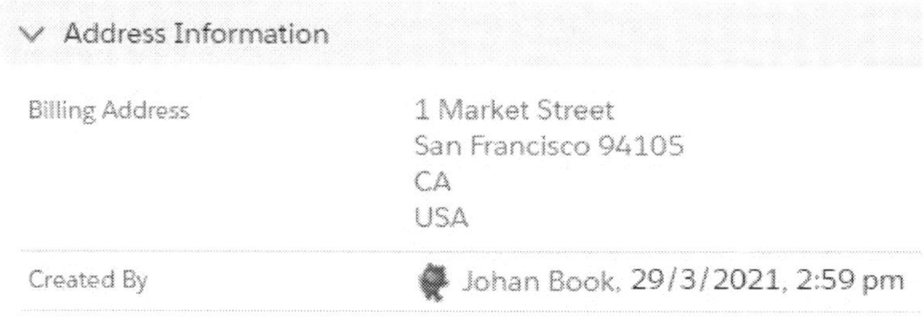

Figure A.12 – Language set to English

Figure A.13 shows the same account view by other users with the language set to Japanese

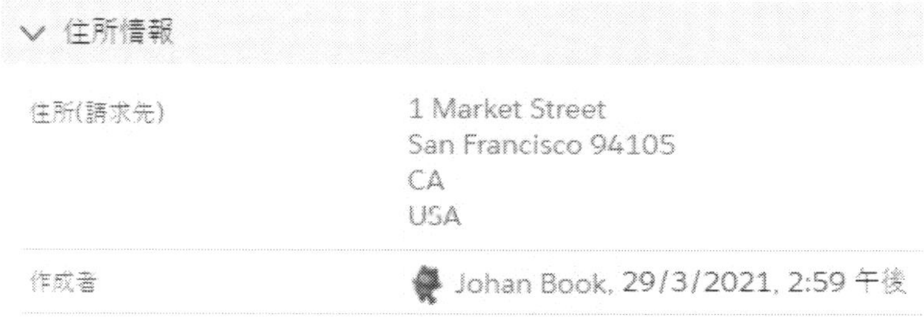

Figure A.13 – Language set to Japanese

4. Currency

Many companies do business in multiple countries meaning amounts and rates often need to be seen converted in records and reports. Salesforce provides a way to do this by enabling multiple currencies, which allows a user to see all records and reports in their preferred personal currency, and provides converted rates also, eliminating the need to do manual conversion work. This also means it is important to have your personal currency accurate in your user detail pages, which reflects:

- When you create an Opportunity, the default currency would be the currency set in your user detail

- When you open an Opportunity with a different currency than your user currency, the system will show a converted value of a currency field, such as Amount, into your own set currency.

Sample:

My currency is set to Euro (EUR), as in *Figure A.14*, the system shows Amount currency conversion for rows 1, 2, and 5 because their Opportunities' currency is not the same as the currency set in my user detail. While Opportunities in rows 3, 4, and 6 are in EUR, which is the same as my currency, so no conversion will be displayed.

Opportunity N... ↑ ∨	Account N... ∨	Stage ∨	Amount
Acme - 600 Widgets	Acme Corp	2 Qualify Opportu...	USD 70,000.0 (EUR 85,909.09)
Action1	System Data	2 Qualify Opportu...	SGD 50,000.00 (EUR 81,000.00)
Alpha-1	Alpha	1 Discovery	EUR 800.00
Alpha-2	Alpha	1 Discovery	EUR 50,000.00
Center-1	Center Plaza	1 Discovery	USD 1,000.0 (EUR 1,227.27)
Center-2	Center Plaza	1 Discovery	EUR 8,000.00

Figure A.14 – Screenshot of a list view to show conversion Amounts

> **Notes**
>
> Currency settings are only available if multicurrency is enabled in your Salesforce org. Once enabled, it cannot be disabled. The conversion rates can be updated by your Salesforce admin to ensure they accurately reflect the current global rates compared to your default corporate currency (often set as that of your HQ).

Setup My Email Setting and Encoding

Salesforce provides the capability to send emails from Salesforce directly. It also allows us to configure a few items related to sending emails directly from the system.

Configure My Email Setting

1. Click your avatar on the upper right corner of your Lightning page
2. Click **Settings** under your name
3. Click > **Email** then click **My Email Settings**

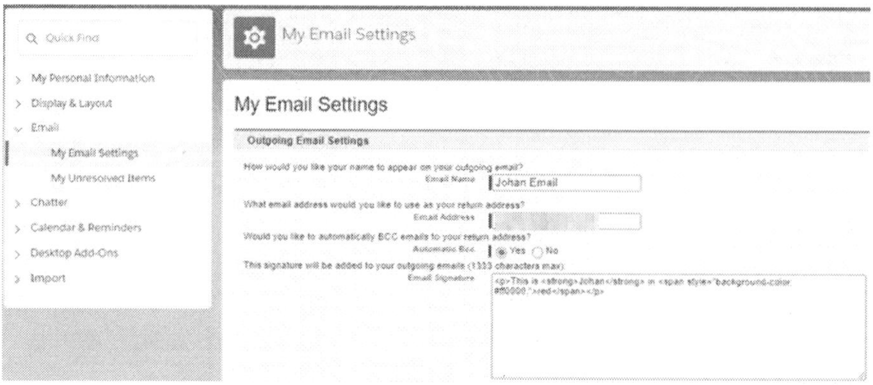

Figure A.15 – My Email Settings

What can you configure in your email settings?

1. You can change your **Email Name**, for example, your name in Salesforce is Gregory Hills, but you want the email sender as Greg Hills, you can change it here.
2. You can set a different **email address** when recipients reply to your email
3. You can always enable **BCC** to yourself for all emails you send out from Salesforce
4. You can add your **email signature**

> **Tips**
>
> You can use formatted text and images for your email signature. Use an online HTML editor to build the signature, such as *https://html-online.com/editor* to build the HTML script.

Configure Email Encoding

Email encoding is useful when you send an email that is not in English characters, such as Chinese, Korean, and Japanese. If the email encoding is not set correctly, the recipients may receive the email message as "*???*" question marks.

Let's configure the encoding:

1. Click your avatar on the upper right corner of your Lightning page
2. Click **Settings** under your name
3. Under **My Personal Information**, click **Language & Time Zone**
4. Change the **Email Encoding** as you need, and select **Unicode (UTF-8)**

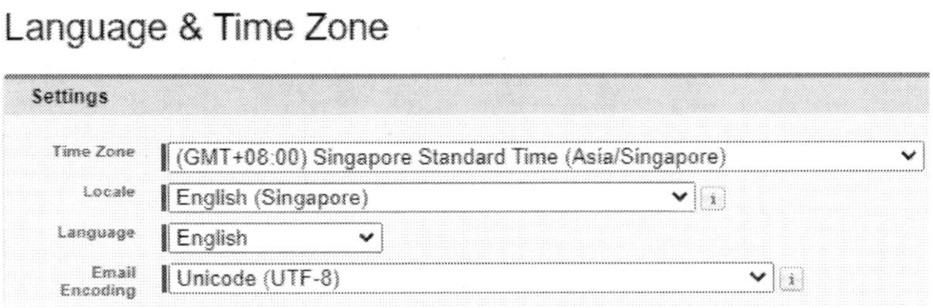

Figure A.16 – Language & Time Zone Settings

Other Setup

There are a few more settings that you can configure for in your personal setup:

- **Approver Settings** – Salesforce has approval features, that your admin needs to configure, in the approver setting, you can set delegated approval, so when you are planning for out of office, you can set your team to approve on your behalf.
- **Record Page Settings** – you can set your preferences on how Activities are displayed on the record page, as Activity Timeline (default) or as Related Lists. Other users will not be impacted by your selection.
- **Set Default Record Type** – if you are aware that Salesforce also has a feature called Record Type, each object can be set up with one or multiple record types, and only your admin can configure that. If there is more than one record type in an object, such as Account (e.g., one for Prospect and one for Customer), your admin will set a default record type for each profile per object. When you enable this, the system will not ask you for a record type selection when creating a new record, the default record type is automatically selected when creating a new record.

You can find all the above setup from your **Settings** under your avatar at the upper right corner.

Summary

In this appendix, we learned things that look simple, but they may impact how you see data in Salesforce correctly, improve your productivity, and be more professional.

A few best practices can be implemented from this appendix:

- Update your avatar with a professional headshot
- Update your user detail correctly, such as time zone, locale, language, and currency
- Not to change your name from what other people know
- Not to use a personal email address
- Configure email setting correctly

APPENDIX: SETTING UP MY SALESFORCE

If you reach this appendix after Chapters 1 to 8, this would be the end of this book, and I hope you have learned many things that can be used and will improve your productivity when working in the Salesforce platform daily. If you have not completed all Chapters 1 to 8, make sure to read through all chapters and practice it accordingly. Thank you!

Made in United States
Orlando, FL
05 November 2026

90231086R00101